Affluence and Activism
Organised Consumers in the Post-War Era

Iselin Theien and Even Lange (eds.)

Unipub forlag
Oslo Academic Press
2004

© Unipub forlag 2004
ISBN 82-7477-186-9

For further information, please contact
Unipub forlag – Oslo Academic Press
Phone: +47 22 85 33 00
Fax: +47 22 85 30 39
E-mail: post@unipub.no

No portion of this book may be copied in violation of copyright law or contrary to agreements with KOPINOR, the interest group for rights holders of creative works in Norway. Any form of unauthorized copying establishes a liability to compensation and confiscation, and is punishable by fine or imprisonment.

Published 2004 by Unipub forlag – Oslo Academic Press
Printed in Norway by AiT e-dit, 2004

Series preface

ISSUES IN CONTEMPORARY HISTORY is a series of publications from the Forum for Contemporary History (FCH) at the University of Oslo. The main focus of the FCH is on the study of changes in political culture as a means towards understanding broader social transformations in the post-World War II period. Our aim is to identify and analyse specific features and patterns of change in the fields of consumer culture, the public sphere, feminism, collective social movements, the welfare state and foreign and security policies in Scandinavian and other Western societies in this period.

Publications in this series will fall into two main categories; edited collections relating to the core interests of the FCH, and monographs primarily based on doctoral dissertations.

The present volume is based on papers presented at the workshop 'Organised Consumers in Twentieth-Century Europe' held at St Hilda's College, Oxford, in September 2003. The editors would like to thank all the participants in this workshop for their valuable contributions to the discussion of the recent history of the consumer movement.

Even Lange and Helge Pharo

Table of Contents

Introduction: Affluence and consumer activism 1
Iselin Theien

I Exit, voice and loyalty: A theoretical framework for exploring consumerism 7
Iselin Theien

II Models of consumer-political action in the twentieth century: Rights, duties and justice 21
Matthew Hilton

III 'Free choice lies at the core of our economic system': A comparative history of post-war British and American consumer organisations. 41
Lawrence Black

IV The surprise of collective action: Consumer mobilisation in France, 1970-1985 61
Gunnar Trumbull

V Corporate efficiency, democratic legitimacy and consumer-political integrity: Norwegian consumer co-operatives, 1970-2002 83
Espen Ekberg and Jon Vatnaland

Contributors 103

Introduction:
Affluence and consumer activism

Iselin Theien

The basic models of consumer organisation were created in a context of scarcity rather than of affluence.[1] One archetype of consumer organisation, the consumer co-operative movement, was established by consumers pooling their resources to buy food in 1844 Britain. By the early twentieth century, the co-operative movement had firmly established itself in Europe as a model for an essentially social form of consumption, organising consumers in democratic, economic associations for the communal purchases of food and other necessities.[2] Two other archetypes of consumer organisation can be found in the USA, in the 1899 National Consumers' League promoting ethical consumption as a means to social ends, and in the 1936 Consumers Union, which emerged out of the 1929 Consumers' Research as an organisation promoting improved information to consumers through comparative testing.[3]

By focusing on developments of the consumer movement in the post-1945 period, this book discusses the fate of the organised consumers in a situation of increasing affluence. To what extent has the consumer movement been able to find new causes after having achieved some of its original

---

[1] On the distinction between consumer organisations of necessity and of affluence, see M. Hilton, *Consumerism in 20th Century Britain: The search for a historical movement* (Cambridge: Cambridge University Press, 2003).
[2] On the co-operative movement, see E. Furlough and C. Strikwerda (eds), *Consumers Against Capitalism? Consumer co-operation in Europe, America and Japan, 1840-1990* (Lanham: Rowman and Littlefield, 1999).
[3] On the National Consumers' League, see L. Storrs, *Civilizing Capitalism* (Chapel Hill: University of North Carolina Press, 2000). For the longer term trends of American consumerism, see L. Cohen, *A Consumers' Republic. The politics of mass consumption in post-war America* (New York: Knopf, 2003).

aims, such as securing ample supplies of food for its members? How well have the original models of consumer organisation been able to cater for the concerns of the more affluent consumers? In short, who are the organised consumers of the affluent post-war societies, and how do they work in order to achieve what aims? These are some of the questions that will be discussed in this book, through selected case studies of different forms of consumer organisation in Britain, the USA, France and Norway.

In considering how the framework for the promotion of consumer interests has developed in the post-war era, the articles in this collection point to several explanations for the forms of organisation that have emerged in the individual countries covered. One set of explanations could be placed in the category of trans-national influences. The co-operative movement could be regarded as a prime example of how a specific model for consumer organisation spread from one country to others, with much of Europe following the lead from the 1844 Rochdale pioneers in England.[4] In the case of the alternative model of private consumer interest organisations, Lawrence Black demonstrates in chapter 3 how elements of this model, as embodied in the US Consumers Union, inspired the creation of the UK Consumers' Association, which, in turn, influenced the creation of similar organisations on the continent and, more recently, in the developing countries, which Matthew Hilton draws attention to in chapter 2.

When looking at the trans-national aspects of the consumer movement, it is equally important to take into account the international organisations that have been established by the various national associations. Since 1895, the consumer co-operative movement has interpreted, negotiated, and reformulated the Rochdale model within the framework of the International Co-operative Alliance (ICA). In a similar fashion, Matthew Hilton analyses the process by which the voluntary consumer associations inspired by the US Consumers Union formed the International Organisation of Consumer Unions (IOCU) in 1960. Through these interna-

---

[4] On the British co-operative movement, see P. Gurney, *Co-operative Culture and the Politics of Consumption in England 1870-1930* (Manchester: Manchester University Press, 1996).

tional organisations, the consumer movement has created a framework for disseminating practices, and they have created a means for promoting their definitions of the consumer interest in other arenas, most notably the UN.

When searching for influences on the different forms of consumer organisations, the broader, international trends within consumption itself also come into the equation. In the articles by Lawrence Black and by Matthew Hilton, the American-inspired consumer unions emerge in part as responses to consumption patterns associated with the increasing affluence of the post-war period, patterns which, in the first place, may arguably also be regarded as an American export to Europe.[5] However, as Espen Ekberg and Jon Vatnaland discuss in their chapter on the Norwegian consumer co-operative movement, this nineteenth-century form of consumer organisation also proved highly flexible in adapting to new patterns of consumption in Scandinavia, as was made apparent by the co-operative venture into fields such as consumer electronics and fast-food restaurants in the 1980s.

In addition to the international influences in terms of common organisational forms and more general patterns of consumption, the development of consumer organisations in individual countries was also shaped in important ways by the specific national political contexts within which they operated. In chapter 4, Gunnar Trumbull attributes an important part of the explanation for the 'surprise of collective action' among French consumers in the 1970s to generous government funding of a broad range of consumer associations, encouraging the development of the consumer movement as a countervailing force to producers. In the case of the US consumer movement, Lawrence Black points out how Ralph Nader perceived the particular legal framework provided by the US anti-trust legislation as fertile ground for consumer activism.

The standing of the different strands of the consumer movement within their larger political and social contexts both nationally and internationally is also a question of how far they have been able to claim legitimacy for their inter-

---

[5] See R.F. Kuisel, *Seducing the French: The dilemma of Americanization* (Berkeley: University of California Press, 1993).

pretations of the consumer interest. There are some obstacles to a particular organisation claiming to represent the consumer interest when compared, for example, with trade unions which have a more clearly defined membership basis, as Gunnar Trumbull shows to have been an argument against the consumer movement in France. Moreover, if a social movement is defined as a form of organisation with an active mass membership participation[6], then both consumer co-operatives and consumer unions have been aware of their shortcomings in this direction in the post-war period.

In the case of the former, Ekberg and Vatnaland argue that although towards the end of the twentieth century Norwegian co-operatives proved able to increase membership numbers, the notion of what was implied by such a membership has undergone significant transformations in the direction of providing more of a customer basis for a business loyalty scheme than the basis for a consumer mass democracy. This tendency from mass movement to more limited forms of membership participation can also be detected in Lawrence Black's description of the Consumers' Association as a class movement (and a middle-class one at that) rather than a mass movement. Nevertheless, Black argues that the US Consumers Union provided a model for envisioning this form of consumer organisation as a social association as well, encouraging collective action among the members.

By applying a different definition of a social movement, focusing on the aims of a given organisation rather than on the nature of its membership, an alternative foundation for consumer organisations' claims to legitimacy can be found. As Matthew Hilton argues, the forms of consumer organisation created in the context of the increasing affluence of Western societies are also displaying characteristics associated with the concept of citizenship. Private consumer unions are not merely working for the rights of individual consumers, but they are also advocating consumer duties in a world of social injustices, for instance through IOCU cam-

---

[6] On the different theories of social movements, see for instance S. Tarrow, *Power in Movement: Social movements and contentious politics* (Cambridge: Cambridge University Press, 1998). On consumerism as a social movement, see R.N. Meyer, *The Consumer Movement. Guardians of the Marketplace* (Boston: Twayne Publishers, 1989)

paigns, which Hilton describes as promoting causes often 'indistinguishable from the demands of the anti-globalisation movement.' Hilton thus demonstrates that private testing organisations such as the Consumers' Association through, arguably, 'selling consumer protection' to their members,[7] have at the same time established a basis for promoting social justice on a global level.

The question of whether the types of consumer organisations associated with affluence are truly social movements, could perhaps be disentangled by allowing for a distinction between social participation and social agenda. It might be argued that in concurrence with wider, organisational trends of the post-war period, the consumer movement has developed in the direction of advocacy and interest representation,[8] weakening participation while at the same time perhaps facilitating the definition of a more clearly defined social agenda.

The question of how affluence has influenced the development of the consumer movement leads into a more fundamental question of how we look at the relationship between consumption and citizenship. As will be discussed in the following chapter, the question of how we understand consumer organisation is intertwined with how we look at consumption as an independent force in society at large. On the one hand, consumption can be seen as a catalyst for an increasing individualisation of society, by directing the attention of citizens towards a material acquisitiveness, but at the same time it could be regarded as a mobilising force for social activism, as made manifest in the various forms adopted by the consumer movement. As such, the history of the consumer movement is highly relevant to the more recent surges of interest in the causes of the perceived decline of social capital in affluent societies.[9] The contributions to this book provide an empirical basis for discussing questions of a more theoreti-

---

[7] S. Franks, 'Selling consumer protection. Competitive strategies of the Consumers' Association, 1957 to 1990' (Oxford M.Phil. thesis, 2000).
[8] See T. Skocpol, *Diminished Democracy: From membership to management in American civic life* (Norman, OK: University of Oklahoma Press, 2003)
[9] R. Putnam, *Bowling Alone. The collapse and revival of American community* (New York: Simon and Schuster, 2000).

cal character concerning the ways in which consumption interacts with social organisation and citizen engagement.

As Gunnar Trumbull argues with reference to the case of the 1970s consumer mobilisation in France, contrary to the expectations of some social scientists,[10] in the real world consumers have proved both willing and able to organise their interests. Moreover, as Ekberg and Vatnaland point out in relation to the developments of the Norwegian consumer cooperative movement in the 1970s, an upswing in consumer activism may very well coincide with increasing affluence.

Taken together, the articles in this book present a case for arguing that the consumer movement has been able to take on board new concerns of Western consumers in the post-war period, through adopting, adapting and experimenting with the original forms of consumer organisation. This book thus challenges the view that the history of the consumer movement in the second half of the twentieth century was one of decline.

---

[10] Most notably M. Olson, *The Logic of Collective Action: Public goods and the theory of groups* (Cambridge: Harvard University Press, 1965).

I

Exit, voice and loyalty: A theoretical framework for exploring consumerism

Iselin Theien

'Consumerism' as a term could be understood to mean at least two different things. In popular debate, as well as by some academics, it has been used to describe a general development of a materialist culture in the affluent Western societies. When regarded as 'the unlimited and general desire for purchased goods and services that define self and social position in advanced market societies', 'consumerism' has acquired negative connotations, for instance when juxtaposed with the declining participation in 'civil society' at large.[1] The underlying rationale here is that affluence and the striving for ever more consumer goods has diverted the interests of Western citizens away from active participation in social organisations and over to individual acquisitiveness. Or, the causal relationship may be turned around, making consumption appear as a rational response, but no solution, to an irrational society. According to Zygmunt Bauman, '[I]t is here, in this predicament of individuals doomed to compensate for the irrationality of their Lebenswelt by resorting to their own wits and acumen, that "consumer society" comes into its own; that life turns into a shopping spree.'[2] In both instances, our roles as consumers

---

[1] Gary Cross, 'Consumerism', in P. Stearns, *Encyclopaedia of European Social History from 1350 to 2000* (New York: Scribner, 2001), pp. 77-88.
[2] Z. Bauman, *Society under siege* (Cambridge: Cambridge University Press, 2002), p. 195.

are cast as a contrast, and possible challenge, to our roles as citizens and social beings.

However, the term 'consumerism' can also be applied with reference to a largely twentieth-century social movement. From the mid-nineteenth century onwards, citizens have organised *qua* consumers in Europe and in the United States, for instance in co-operatives and more activist consumer organisations ranging from the American National Consumers' League at the dawn of the twentieth century to strands of the present-day anti-globalisation movement.[3] When talking about 'consumerism' in such a context, the term denotes the organised promotion of the consumer interest.

The difference between the two meanings of the term 'consumerism' can be regarded as stretching beyond the strictly semantic level. Whether celebrated or lamented, the understanding of 'consumerism' as the growth of material acquisitiveness directs our attention towards the individual shopper. It is the individual who strives for ever more consumer goods, and in the criticism of 'consumerism', this ambition is regarded as a way of diverting attention and resources from civic engagement. In contrast, the second definition of the term 'consumerism' points to consumption as a spur to social organisation. A wide range of organisations has been formed around issues relating to consumption in the twentieth century, such as the need for basic foodstuffs and concerns about safety, health and the wider social implications of the production process. As such, consumption appears as a fertile ground for civic engagement rather than as the culprit in a story of declining participation in Western societies.

A central question that presents itself through these two different definitions of 'consumerism' is thus what impact the broadening access to consumer goods has on civic life in affluent societies. In order to approach this admittedly broad question, it may be time to take a second look at the American economist and political scientist Albert O. Hirschman's *Exit, Voice and Loyalty.* Responses to decline in firms, or-

---

[3] On the continuities of consumer activism, see P. Maclachlan and F. Trentmann, 'Civilising markets: Traditions of consumer politics in twentieth-century Britain, Japan and the United States', in M. Bevir and F. Trentmann (eds), *Markets in Historical Contexts: Ideas and Politics in the Modern World* (Cambridge: Cambridge University Press, 2003).

ganizations and states.[4] This provides a theoretical framework for understanding in what situations consumers may choose to engage in public debate and collective action rather than to withdraw to an individualist acquisitiveness. In short, exit, voice, and loyalty are the three principal options that consumers are faced with when they encounter problems in the market,[5] and through this repertoire of reactions the individual shopper may find reason to enter into collaboration with other consumers.

Exit

The first of the recuperation mechanisms for consumers and citizens unhappy about the state of affairs that Hirschman introduces is that of exit. The traditional economist would think of exit as the natural way to express dissatisfaction in the market place. Customers who are unhappy about a producer will simply take their business elsewhere. Eventually, when enough customers stop buying a product, the exit mechanism will feed back to the firm, which will then change its product without ever having heard the actual voice of the individual consumer.

The exit mechanism thus requires that consumers have a real choice between competing producers, which is a problematic assumption for several reasons. For example, Hirschman asks us to consider instances where the consumer only has a choice between a number of less than perfect products. Competition between the producers of such products would be real enough, but by only exercising exit as their way of showing dissatisfaction, the end result for con-

---

[4] A.O. Hirschman, *Exit, Voice and Loyalty. Responses to decline in firms, organizations and states* (Cambridge MA: Harvard University Press, 1970). Elements of Hirschman's theory have been applied to explain consumer behaviour by political scientists such as T. Bjørklund, 'Forbrukerinnflytelse på dagligvareforsyningen' (Report to Nordisk Ministerråd, Oslo, 1984) and V. Pestoff, 'Exit, voice and collective action in Swedish consumer policy', in *Journal of consumer policy*, 11/1988, pp. 1-27.
[5] These three categories need not be regarded as exclusive. Guy Bajoit has suggested that 'apathy' may be added as a fourth option to Hirschman's scheme, see G. Bajoit, 'Exit, voice, loyalty ... and apathy. Les réactions individuelles au mécontentement', in *Revue francais de sociologie*, XXIX, 1988, pp. 325-345.

sumers would be less than satisfactory no matter which product they chose. Also, under such circumstances, the exits of a given number of consumers moving between firms may balance each other out. A firm would have no way of knowing that its customers were dissatisfied and so ceasing to buy its products if, at the same time, it was gaining a similar number of new customers who were equally dissatisfied with the products of a competing firm. A more common problem in relation to the exercise of exit is that of producers establishing virtual monopolies in their designated fields. When there only exists one supplier of a product that consumers cannot comfortably do without for an extended period, they are effectively deprived of the exit option for expressing their dissatisfaction.

The discussion of how far the exit option yields any real power to consumers is thus closely linked to the discussion of how far capitalism delivers its promise of free competition. The concept of exit only makes sense where consumers have a real choice, either by ceasing to buy a product altogether or, more commonly, by switching to another supplier. Even though the exit option is silent in nature, for our discussion it is important to look at how consumers themselves have approached the issue of capitalist competition. Then we need to look beyond the anonymous demand-side of the market economy model and turn to the vocal representatives of consumer interests.

The historian Frank Trentmann has provided an assessment of the shift from what he describes as a radical-liberal to a social-democratic vision of consumption and citizenship in Britain, in which he ascribes a central position to consumer activists and organisations in the gradual replacement of a consumption policy of free trade for one of increased regulation in the wake of the First World War.[6] When the focus of historical analysis is turned from traditional policy-makers and impersonal customers to the vocal representatives of consumer interests, it becomes clearer how consumers have perceived the exit mechanism.

In the decades leading up to the First World War, Trentmann demonstrates how consumers of different back-

---

[6] F. Trentmann, 'Bread, milk and democracy', in M. Daunton and M. Hilton (eds), *The Politics of Consumption. Material Culture and Citizenship in Europe and America* (Oxford: Berg, 2001).

grounds rallied to the banner of Free Trade as the preferred solution to providing the population with essential foodstuffs as cheaply as possible. As such, consumers declared their preference for the mechanisms of the market over political solutions, in particular the forms of protectionism pursued by other nations at the time, in order to promote a radical liberalism which was regarded as superior in rational as well as in moral terms. For, as the British Free Traders saw it, international competition was primarily a means of preventing poverty and starvation among the broad masses of consumers, and as a way 'to insulate society against materialism, which, like capital trusts, was traced to the selfish culture of protectionism.'[7]

In the trajectory of the radical liberalism of British consumers, the consumer co-operative movement in Norway proved remarkably confident that free trade represented the superior economic system.[8] The Norwegian co-operative movement, which had its membership base among workers and farmers, continued to defend market competition throughout the 1930s, in an international and domestic climate favouring increased political regulation of the economy. As in the British case, Norwegian consumer activists defended free markets in a language of rationality as well as of morality. As the co-operators saw it, free competition would provide consumers with the best possible access to food stuffs and other goods by encouraging rational production. In addition, the co-operators regarded any far-reaching political regulation of the market as an infringement of democratic ideals, inspired by nothing less than the totalitarian policies of Nazi Germany. Thus, the Norwegian co-operators actively engaged in the 1930s domestic debate to defend a liberal economy where consumers would be free to exercise their exit option.

The Free Trade ethos guiding the early British consumer movement as well as the Norwegian consumer co-operatives is an important reminder that the notion of 'consumer choice' so popular with neo-liberals of the latter part

---

[7] Ibid., p. 135.
[8] I. Theien, 'Socialism, liberalism or political neutrality? The balancing act of the consumer co-operatives in inter-war Norway', in *Journal of Co-operative Studies* 3/2002, pp. 167-182.

of the twentieth century does not represent the only defence of the exit mechanism in free markets. The reasons why the British and the Norwegian consumer movements favoured markets over politics in the first decades of the twentieth century were very different from the individualist outlook of the neo-liberals of the later decades of it. As Trentmann has pointed out in his studies of the British advocates of Free Trade, this radical-liberal agenda was embedded in a concern for civil society at large. Through participation in free markets, consumers were expected to act as good citizens rather than as individual customers simply shopping around for the best deal. In this scenario, political regulation of the economy appeared as more of an obstacle to than a vehicle for the aim of popular participation and civic engagement in matters concerning consumption.

The contemporary anti-globalisation movement has taken up elements of this early, radical consumerist agenda. Although banners for Free Trade would be hard to come by in an anti-globalisation demonstration march, the call for the protection of consumers' right to exit can be heard among the plethora of the new activist voices. For a start, it is notable that one of the sections of the proclaimed anti-globalisation 'bible', Naomi Klein's *No Logo*, carries the title 'No Choice'.[9] Here, she analyses what she describes as the 'assault on choice' committed by multi-national companies forever merging into larger units and wiping out competition. As a telling example of this tendency, she presents the business strategies of the American coffee chain Starbucks. According to Klein, the Starbucks strategy is to 'drop "clusters" of outlets in urban areas already dotted with cafés and espresso-bars... The idea is to saturate an area with stores until the coffee competition is so fierce that sales drop even in individual Starbucks outlets.'[10] In this way, consumer choice becomes illusory; to paraphrase Henry Ford, we are then left with the choice of having any coffee we would like, as long as it is Starbucks.

---

[9] N. Klein: *No Logo. Taking aim at the brand bullies* (New York: Picador, 1999), p. 129.
[10] ibid., p. 136.

When big business distorts markets as illustrated by the case of Starbucks, consumers are deprived of the exit option of taking their business elsewhere. Klein's criticism of giant corporations like Starbucks, Nike and Shell is reminiscent of earlier consumerist agendas in pointing out how monopolies leave consumers in a position of 'No Choice'. And here, we find ourselves in the midst of one of Hirschman's analytical points. According to conventional economic wisdom, monopolies are indeed evil because they preclude competition. However, Hirschman brings our attention to the possibility that monopolies by the same token can open the way to a different form of consumer influence. When the exit option is closed off, consumers can turn to the voice option instead. In this light, we may regard the growth of the anti-globalisation movement as a reaction to the monopolist tendencies of the multi-national companies Naomi Klein is attacking.

In discussing whether consumption is fostering or hindering civic engagement, the examples of consumers actively defending their exit option are interesting for two reasons. Firstly, they show that from a consumer perspective, the defence of the exit mechanism is not necessarily guided by an individualist acquisitiveness, but rather by a concern for empowering consumers of all social backgrounds. Secondly, these examples show that although consumers may appear to be individualist shoppers under a capitalist system, they are also capable of organising to defend their rights as customers when they perceive the exit mechanism to be under threat. Such an articulation of consumer interests leads us on to the next of Hirschman's concepts, that of voice.

Voice

Voice is the mechanism that is most commonly attributed to the political sphere. Hirschman defines it as 'any attempt at all to change, rather than to escape from, an objectionable state of affairs.'[11] Most typically, the citizens of a democracy will use their voice when they vote in general elections. Here, it is also important to include another of Hirschman's considerations in the equation, namely the relationship be-

---

[11] Hirschman, *Exit, Voice and Loyalty*, p. 30.

tween voice and exit. Where the cost of exit is high, the use of voice is more likely, unless the cost of voice is significant as well. For instance, the cost of exit is high for most members of a nation state, in the sense that moving to another country often involves considerable personal and economic consequences. In a democracy, then, it is likely that the citizens will use their vote or other forms of political action to try to change any given 'objectionable state of affairs', whereas in dictatorships the costs of voice will often prevent political action, and for some to the point where even the high costs associated with exit by escaping the country seem relatively small.

In the market, where the cost of exit is usually low, the use of voice may appear to be less applicable. Whereas the use of exit normally demands minimal effort in the market place, the use of voice is more troublesome and requires greater skill and effort. Nevertheless, Hirschman noted in 1970 that the consumer voice had become increasingly audible in his contemporary America, reaching a level where there was talk of a 'consumer revolution'.[12] Hirschman credits the campaigns of the American consumer advocate Ralph Nader with an entrepreneurship paving the way for this revolution.

Ralph Nader's entry onto the stage of consumer activism certainly has the ring of entrepreneurship about it. As a freelance writer with an education in law, Nader launched an attack on the mighty car industry with the book *Unsafe at Any Speed: the designed-in dangers of the American automobile* in 1965. The main target of Nader's attack was General Motors, which was accused of jeopardising safety in the production of the Corvair sports car. Quite explicitly, Nader placed the blame for the lack of auto safety on the shortcomings of markets and politics alike, in arguing that the public had 'never been supplied the information nor offered the quality of competition to enable it to make effective demands through the marketplace and through government for a safe, non-polluting and efficient automobile that can be produced economically.'[13]

---

[12] ibid., p. 42.
[13] R. Nader, *Unsafe at Any Speed: The designed-in dangers of the American automobile* (New York: Grossman, 1965, p. xi.)

As such, Nader's use of his consumer voice can be understood as a response to 'an objectionable state of affairs', where neither the use of exit in markets nor the traditional use of voice in politics had proved to be an adequate instrument for promoting the consumer interest. In his follow-up to the attack on General Motors, Nader joined forces with political actors to press for an auto safety reform measure in the legal system, resulting in the introduction of federal laws providing a better framework for the interests of car consumers by the beginning of the 1970s. He also formed a number of professional legal and other consumer interest organisations, most famous of which is perhaps Public Citizen, set up in 1971.[14]

Innovative as Nader's attack on General Motors was, it ties in with a longer tradition of journalistic exposés of business wrong-doings against consumers in America. This tradition has been traced back to the beginning of the twentieth century, when Upton Sinclair exposed questionable practices of the meat industry in *The Jungle*.[15] Although a work of fiction, *The Jungle* triggered independent investigations into the meat industry, which, in turn, led to the introduction of legislation on meat inspection and wholesome food.[16] The Great Depression carried with it a new surge of consumer-as-journalist voices, most prominent among whom were the economist Stuart Chase and the engineer Frederick Schlink.[17] Chase and Schlink also anticipated the consumer activism of Ralph Nader in another, important fashion, namely by using the publicity they had achieved as writers to form a consumer organisation, the Consumers' Research Inc. In 1936, a

---

[14] D. Bollier, *Citizen Action and Other Big Ideas: A history of Ralph Nader and the modern consumer movement* (Washington, DC: Center for Study of Responsive Law, 1989). C. McCarry, *Citizen Nader* (London: Jonathan Cape Ltd, 1972).
[15] U. Sinclair: *The Jungle* (Harmondsworth: Penguin, 1986 (1906)) See: M. Hilton and M. Daunton: 'Material Politics: An introduction', in *The Politics of Consumption*, p. 19.
[16] R. Herrmann and R.N. Mayer, 'U.S. Consumer Movement: History and dynamics', in S. Brobeck, R. N. Mayer and R. O. Herrmann (eds), *Encyclopaedia of the Consumer Movement* (Santa Barbara: ABC-CLIO, 1997), p. 586.
[17] S. Chase and F.J. Schlink, *Your Money's Worth: A study in the waste of the consumer's dollar* (London: Jonathan Cape, 1927).

more activist spin-off group from this organisation formed what was to become America's leading consumer organisation, the Consumers Union.[18]

The link from these early American consumer advocates to Ralph Nader is in some respects quite direct. For instance, a Center on Auto Safety was created as a joint venture between Nader and the Consumers Union to monitor the safety regulations passed in the wake of *Unsafe at Any Speed*. And the next industry Nader turned to was the meat packing one of Sinclair's *The Jungle*, which resulted in the 1967 passage of the first Wholesome Meat Act since the meat inspection bill inspired by Sinclair nearly fifty years earlier.[19] These three examples of American consumer activism are also linked by their apparent successes, in initiating pro-consumer legislation in the case of Sinclair and Nader, and in building lasting organisations in the case of Stuart and Schlink in the 1930s and of Nader in the 1970s. As such, these consumer activists provide empirical support for one of Hirschman's concluding theoretical points in relation to exit and voice, namely that the introduction of an underused mechanism can prove highly efficient because of the shock effect it produces.[20] In the realm of politics, the exit of a politician will often serve as a powerful expression of protest, and in the realm of markets, the consumer voice can be highly audible against the background of silent exits.

Loyalty

The third concept Hirschman introduces in his analysis is that of loyalty, which he explains along the lines of the special attachment an individual forms to an institution based on the expectation that, in the long run, the institution will do more right than wrong.[21] In the case of the nation state, for instance, there is clearly an element of loyalty to the state at work, which helps to raise the barrier to exit for its citizens. Rather than exiting a state, citizens who feel a

---

[18] L.B. Glickman, 'The Strike in the Temple of Consumerism', in *Journal of American History*, 88:1, 2001, pp. 99-128.
[19] See D. Bollier, *Citizen Action and Other Big Ideas*.
[20] Hirschman, *Exit, Voice and Loyalty*, p. 125.
[21] ibid., p. 78.

sense of loyalty will often stay on to try to change affairs, because they care about the future of the country whether or not they will continue living there themselves. To revert to the case of the market, loyalty could also play a part when individual consumers consider their options. A link between these two cases can be found in instances where citizens choose nationally produced goods over foreign imports regardless of whether the latter would appear to offer more straightforward material benefits to the individual consumer.

In an article with the telling title of 'When interests are not preferences: the cautionary tale of Japanese consumers', Steven K. Vogel explores some possible explanations as to the commonly recognised producer-oriented bias of post-war Japan.[22] He warns us against making an automatic equation between the loyalty so clearly displayed by Japanese consumers towards the interests of national producers and any irrationality or weakness on their behalf. In fact, Vogel points out that Japanese consumers in many respects have been well organised and articulate in the post-war era, for instance through the Japanese housewives' federation. Shufuren. Since its establishment in 1948, Shufuren has fought a number of successful battles on behalf of Japanese consumers in matters relating to safety and the labelling of different products, while at the same time quite literally accepting the need to pay a price for national protectionism. Consequently, Vogel suggests that the Japanese policy of protecting national industries rather than promoting competition to encourage lower prices has been actively supported by domestic consumers.

The story of Japanese consumers is interesting because it illustrates one of Hirschman's points in relation to the concept of loyalty, namely that while loyalty will raise the barrier to exit, it will by the same token encourage the use of voice. This could be regarded as another explanation for why we often associate voice with the realm of politics rather than with that of the market; the loyalty we feel towards political institutions such as the national government triggers the use of voice when we are worried about the direction in which it is heading. In contrast, we often feel less loyal to

---

[22] S. K. Vogel, 'When interests are not preferences: The cautionary tale of Japanese consumers', in *Comparative Politics* 2/1999, pp. 187-207.

an actor in the market place; if a firm goes into decline or completely disappears, consumers often simply don't care as long as a replacement can be found. However, there are notable exceptions to this generalisation, too. A clear example of a market institution that has attracted high levels of loyalty from consumers is the co-operative movement, which rapidly expanded throughout Europe from the mid nineteenth century onwards. By the end of the First World War, the co-operative movement had reached its zenith, with membership rates that encompassed 35 percent of the British and 20 percent of the German population.[23]

The consumer co-operatives are a peculiar combination of business enterprise and democratic organisation. The model for the co-operative movement was provided by the Rochdale Pioneers, who opened a store for the sale of basic foodstuffs in Britain in 1844. The Rochdale pioneers established the principle that the members of a co-operative society, through buying an equal share of the business, would jointly control the store and share any surplus on the basis of how much each member had purchased during a year. As such, there existed a material incentive for loyalty to the store for its members, in the sense that the more money they spent there, the greater the share of the surplus they would be entitled to. Also, by providing the capital for the store through buying a share, each member would have an interest in the survival of the store. Moreover, due to the democratic principle on which the co-operative society was founded, there was a strong incentive for members to use their voice in the election of the best possible officers to run the stores.

However, the loyalty generated by the co-operative societies cannot be reduced entirely to the materialist considerations of the members. Despite an ideology partly based on a vision of class harmony and resting on the twin heritage of liberalism and socialism, the co-operative movement was to a large extent a working-class phenomenon. This meant that for many of the members, shopping in the co-operative stores was an expression of class solidarity. In his history of the Brit-

---

[23] E. Furlough and C. Strikwerda (eds), *Consumers against Capitalism? Consumer Co-operation in Europe, America and Japan, 1840-1990* (Lanham: Rowman and Littlefield, 1999) p. 19.

ish consumer co-operatives, Peter Gurney describes the co-operative stores 'as a defining feature of working-class community and neighbourhood life which generated fierce loyalties.' An expression of this sentiment is captured in a quote from an anonymous women writing in her local co-operative newspaper in 1913, where she passed on a saying of her mother: 'Keep true to the store and the store will keep true to you.'[24]

The loyalty of the consumer co-operators to their organisation can be regarded as mirroring that of citizens to a nation state or that of the members of a political party in that the co-operative movement represented an independent and integrated world for social belonging. Indeed, at the beginning of the twentieth century, intellectuals such as Charles Gide and Leonard Woolf envisaged that the co-operative movement could form the basis of a new social order in the shape of a 'Co-operative Republic'. The utopian vision of the co-operative movement as an alternative to other forms of political organisation persisted in pockets up until the inter-war period. As late as 1927, Gide replied in the negative to his own question of whether he had provided *'une revue nécrologique'* of the attempts to form independent co-operative colonies outside of the existing political order. Instead, Gide expressed a belief that communitarian and co-operative societies in the future could provide the basis for a social order similar to that of the religious societies of the medieval era.[25]

The co-operative movement thus provides an example of how consumers, either due to a shared, utopian vision of a 'Co-operative Republic' or on the basis of class solidarity, have been able to form an organisation invoking the mechanism of loyalty. The co-operative movement can also be used to illustrate one, final point in relation to the discussion on exit versus voice, namely that there is a 'third solution' available to consumers, which goes beyond the use of exit and voice. Through the co-operative movement, consumers have formed an organisation for promoting their interests largely independent of private market actors and political institutions

---

[24] P. Gurney, *Co-operative Culture and the Politics of Consumption in England, 1870-1930* (Manchester: Manchester University Press, 1996), p. 62-64.
[25] C. Gide, *Les Colonies Communistes et Coopératives* (Paris: Association pour l'enseignement de la cooperation, 1928).

alike. As such, the co-operative movement could be understood as a consumerist reaction to unresponsive markets or political actors, or, to stick to Hirschman's terms, the co-operative movement has served as an alternative when the use of exit and voice has failed as means of channelling the consumer interest.

We could thus understand the consumers' choice of exit, voice or loyalty in terms of the responsiveness of the institutions with which they are dealing. If the impersonal market mechanism fails to absorb the message of consumers exiting, they may choose to turn to the use of voice. However, if their voices go equally unheard, be it by the market actors or by the state, the creation of alternative institutions like the consumer co-operatives may present itself as a better choice. In relation to the wider discussion of how we are to understand 'consumerism', as a term describing an essentially individualist acquisitiveness or as a term denouncing the organised promotion of the consumer interest, the principal strength of Hirschman's model is that it draws our attention to the strong incentives that exist for consumers to articulate their interests when markets function less than perfectly. And as such, it can serve as an important reminder that consumption does not equal passivity, but may just as well serve as a fertile ground for social and political activism.

II

Models of consumer-political action in the twentieth century: Rights, duties and justice

Matthew Hilton

Organisations of consumers are hardly a phenomenon specific to the twentieth century. From the late-eighteenth century women arranged to boycott slave-grown sugar and, in the nineteenth they acted as regular customers to pressurise local shopkeepers to support such political campaigns as Chartism. Food riots have been interpreted as clear manifestations of a consumer consciousness and, most prominently, Rochdale-based consumers' co-operation spread throughout Britain and beyond, particularly in northern and western Europe. Yet it is nevertheless clear that over the last one hundred years our roles as consumers have become increasingly tied to socio-political institutions and to citizens' relationships with the state and civil society. Beginning in the 1880s, a Consumers' League was set up in Britain only to soon falter and then be taken up far more successfully in the United States. These organisations of civic and philanthropic-minded women taught middle-class shoppers about the labour conditions that went into the products they purchased in the flourishing department stores. 'White lists' of fairly manufactured goods soon returned to Europe and in the first decade of the twentieth century Consumers' Leagues appeared in France, the Netherlands, Switzerland, Germany and Belgium.[1] Shortages during the First World War, followed by fluctuating prices and economic hardship in the 1920s and 1930s, further led to a politicisation of price and the articulation of various rights of consumers to basic needs. Again, women as consumers directly involved themselves in political action, often through a growing number of non-feminist middle-class groups, but also in unity with their working-class husbands through various labour and trade union organisations.

These poverty-inspired bodies stand in contrast to the growth of consumer testing associations linked to post-Second World War affluence. Taking the lead from the US Consumers Union, founded in 1936 following a split with Consumers' Research (founded in 1929), several consumer groups emerged in Europe beginning in France with the Union fédérale de la consommation in 1951, followed by the Nederlandse Consumentenbond (1953), the UK Consumers' Association (1956) and the Belgian Association des Consommateurs (1957), as well as several state-sponsored bodies such as the Norwegian Forbrukerrådet (1953) and the Swedish Statens Konsumentråd (1957).[2] In the 1960s and 1970s, European states were galvanised by such movements to introduce a range of consumer protection measures at both national and EU level. From the 1980s, various commentators have pointed to a perceived backlash against consumer protection from pro-business governments, but consumers themselves have continued to organise and participate in civil society. Consumers' unions have expanded across the globe, supervised by the International Organisation of Consumers' Unions (IOCU, now Consumers International) and an ever-expanding array of single-issue pressure groups have worked to challenge the structures and direction of economic globalisation.

Organised consumers, then, have been a persistent, if diverse, presence across twentieth-century Europe. Scholarship on the subject, though, is only just beginning to emerge, except-

---

[1] M-E. Chessel, 'Aux origines de la consommation engagée: La Ligue sociale d'acheteurs, 1902-1914', in *Vingtième siècle. Revue d'histoire*, forthcoming.
[2] S. Brobeck, R. N. Mayer and R. O. Herrmann (eds), *Encyclopaedia of the Consumer Movement* (Santa Barbara: ABC-CLIO, 1997).

ing an earlier body of work on consumers' co-operation.[3] It has been difficult to set out models of development of consumer organisation or consumer politics, although a recent spate of edited works has emerged, less influenced perhaps by an older moral discussion of the vices and virtues of consumption.[4] Examining the potential of consumption as a political movement, rather than as a moral discourse (though the two are hardly separable), has enabled a literature to emerge that sees in consumer organisation a history of sometimes radical politics with much to suggest for discussions of the consumer interest today. Consumer organisation has been about much more than acquisitive individualism (as various historians have suggested regarding both co-operation and affluent consumer testing bodies) and has often been a reflection of the political rights and duties of a nation's citizens. The problem remains, however, that the definition of the consumer interest is almost infinite in its scope and any history of consumer organisations must acknowledge the lack of unity in the myriad politicisations of the consumer'.

In what follows I will review some of the literature on the history of consumer organisations, as well as offering a case study of Britain to problematise some of the key issues. What is clear is that questions concerning the relationship between the citizen and the consumer have dominated both the agendas of historians and of organisations themselves. How that relationship has manifested itself has also depended upon the types of goods being discussed and there is a clear distinction to be made between a consumer politics based on necessity and one based on affluence, though the differences ought not to be over-emphasised. The classic

---

[3] For an overview see E. Furlough and C. Strikwerda (eds), *Consumers Against Capitalism? Consumer cooperation in Europe, North America and Japan, 1840-1990* (Oxford: Rowman and Littlefield, 1999).
[4] S. Strasser, C. McGovern and M. Judt (eds), *Getting and Spending: European and American consumer societies in the twentieth century* (Cambridge, Cambridge University Press, 1998); V. de Grazia and E. Furlough (eds), *The Sex of Things: Gender and consumption in historical perspective* (Berkeley: University of California Press, 1996); M. Daunton and M. Hilton (eds), *The Politics of Consumption: Material culture and citizenship in Europe and America* (Oxford: Berg, 2001); L. B. Glickman (ed.), *Consumer Society in American History: A Reader* (Ithaca: Cornell University Press, 1999).

concerns of liberal democracy (the rights and duties of citizenship, together with the responsibilities of the individual and the state) have dominated this discussion and a number of historians have tended to see in early-twentieth century consumer organisations a focus on the consuming duties of citizens. Post-1945, consumerism has been positioned as much more individualistic and rights-based. But as will be seen in the case study of Britain and in the overview of certain international developments, this is too simple a model and what has been observable over recent decades has been a focus on issues of social justice within many consumer organisations, whether co-operative, ethical or even those ostensibly concerned with the value for money of different branded goods.

It is the scholarship on the United States that has led the way in the history of politicised consumerism, or at least it is there that the study of consumer activism has been most developed. In the latest, and perhaps most important, examination of the phenomenon, Lizabeth Cohen has offered a clear chronological model for the development of consumer politics and consumer citizenship.[5] To begin with, and following the work of other scholars, she argues that the late-nineteenth and early-twentieth century campaigns for workers' rights to a decent standard of living (a 'living wage') and limits to the power of trusts and combines amounted to a 'first wave' of consumer activism.[6] The New Deal period further mobilised and institutionalised 'citizen consumers' who fought for their individual rights at the same time as using their economic power for the greater good of the US economic recovery. At the same time, a competing ideal, that of the 'purchaser consumer' was promoted by business and political groups which celebrated the consumer as an individual shopper whose self-interested actions would aid aggregate purchasing power. In the 1940s, first during war and later during recovery, the two competing notions were combined in the 'purchaser as citizen' model, a type of compro-

---

[5] L. Cohen, *A Consumer's Republic: The politics of mass consumption in postwar America* (New York: Knopf, 2003). See also her 'Citizens and consumers in the United States in the century of mass consumption', in Daunton and Hilton, *Politics of Consumption*, pp. 203-221.
[6] L. B. Glickman, *A Living Wage: American workers and the making of consumer society* (Ithaca: Cornell University Press, 1997).

mise as personal interests were held to serve the national interest, since economic growth depended upon the dynamism of mass consumption. This was the age of Cohen's 'Consumers' Republic', where material acquisition was celebrated as the very essence of the American way of life. From the 1970s, though, de-regulation, 'Reaganomics' and the ascendancy of anti-consumer citizen forces resulted in the creation of the 'Consumerized Republic', a society in which our roles as consumers, citizens, taxpayers and voters have been combined, promoting a view of life where all market transactions and government policies are judged according to narrow criteria of individual satisfaction.

This model, roughly tracing a transition from a politically richer and more idealistic consumer citizenship to a more impoverished notion of the consumer as a mere acquisitive individual, fits with earlier interpretations of consumerism in the United States. It builds on other investigations of the New Deal and war-time periods and of the origins of comparative-testing consumerism when Consumers' Research took account of the labour conditions that lay behind the production of the tested branded commodities.[7] More importantly, Cohen's account confirms the long-established unease of many American scholars with the culture of abundance. From the 1950s, liberal-left and Frankfurt School-inspired critiques of mass consumption emerged in a series of bestselling popular studies which have inspired a generation of historians who have, long after the turn to consumption as a serious arena of academic scrutiny, continued to disparage organised consumerism. Consumers have not been recognised as an active political force and organisations such as the comparative-testing Consumers Union have been dismissed as tending 'to reinforce both the individualism and

---

[7] M. Jacobs, '"How about some meat?" The Office of Price Administration, consumption politics, and state-building from the bottom up, 1941-1946', in *Journal of American History*, 84, 1997, pp. 910-941; M. Jacobs, 'Democracy's third estate: New Deal politics and the construction of a "consuming public"', in *International Labour and Working-Class History*, 55, 1999, pp. 27-51; C. McGovern, 'Consumption and citizenship in the United States, 1900-1940', in Strasser et al., *Getting and Spending*, pp. 37-58; L. Glickman, 'The strike in the temple of consumption: Consumer activism and twentieth-century American political culture', in *Journal of American History*, 88:1, 2001, pp. 99-128.

materialism of American consumption.'[8] As will be seen below, it is more difficult to arrive at such a conclusion of organised consumerism in Europe, but the benefit of Cohen's approach is her acknowledgement of the highly nuanced effects of consumption during the heyday of her 'Consumers' Republic.' Although arguing that political consumerism largely failed, she does acknowledge the significant influence of Ralph Nader's aggressive third wave consumerism of the 1960s and 1970s. And she readily admits both the positive and negative aspects of consumption, be it in the shopping malls of suburbia which opened up spaces for women, though in a highly circumscribed manner, or through the civil rights campaigns of African Americans who used consumption to highlight inequality while at the same time bringing them more firmly within the realm of commerce. The Consumers' Republic brought real benefits for many Americans and from the late-1940s to the 1960s, the act of purchasing, and the attendant rights surrounding this activity, did seem to offer a means for both fuelling self-interest and the larger cause of revitalising America in the economic, social and political spheres. For all this, though, Cohen concludes on a negative note, arguing that mass marketing, political polling and housing segregation encouraged consumers and citizens to focus on narrower and more localised issues, only considering national policies in terms of self-interest. Attempts were made by a Nader-inspired consumer movement to re-politicise consumption but these were defeated by the end of the 1970s and an ascendant neo-liberalism ensured the subsequent divorce of consumption and citizenship.

The questions are, therefore, whether such a model can be applied to other countries and whether similar trajectories of an increasing separation between the consumer and the citizen can be traced. We might ask of Cohen's model whether there was ever such a coherent model of citizenship in the earlier period. Did the campaigns for the living wage, the activities of the Consumers' Leagues and the demands led by groups such as the League of Women Shoppers (founded in New York in 1935) represent a viable political alternative? And of the later period, in the transition to af-

---

[8] G. Cross, *An All-Consuming Century: Why commercialism won in modern America* (New York: Columbia University Press), pp. 134-135.

fluence, did comparative-testing consumer bodies play such a minor role, especially given the expansion of US consumer protection legislation in the 1960s and 1970s which had been similarly demanded by consumer activists across the developed world? If we are, first of all, to accept this model's applicability to the United States, can we then suggest that it works for Britain and Europe as well?

Certainly, there is much to commend it, and we might posit a similar story of the changing nature of rights and duties over the last one hundred years. It could easily be held that consumption was earlier conceived of as an other-directed expression of duties, in which the rights of consumers were seen to be held in common, most famously perhaps in E. P. Thompson's moral economy where the food riot is argued to be the articulation of a 'highly-sensitive consumer-consciousness'.[9] And in the second half of the twentieth century it could be similarly concluded that affluent, organised, comparative-testing based consumerism encouraged individuals to think only in terms of value for money. When these concerns were expressed politically, they were about defending the rights of the individual to consume, such that subsequent generations of politicians have appealed to voters as consumers in terms of the right to individual choice rather than the duties to think of the whole range of citizenship-based issues which relate to our consuming lives. It is a tempting conclusion, but in one of the few comparative studies of organised consumer politics, it has been argued that national political and cultural traditions remain crucial. The success or otherwise of consumer politics has instead rested on 'the ability of movements to frame their objectives in ways that complement or contribute to broader cultural norms and prevailing ideas about democracy and political economy.'[10] Thus, it is likely that the history of organised consumers can follow rather different trajectories from one

---

[9] E. P. Thompson, 'The moral economy of the English crowd in the eighteenth century', in *Past and Present*, 50, 1971, pp. 76-136.
[10] P. Maclachlan and F. Trentmann, 'Civilising markets: Traditions of consumer politics in twentieth-century Britain, Japan and the United States', in M. Bevir and F. Trentmann (eds), *Markets in Historical Contexts: Ideas and Politics in the Modern World* (Cambridge: Cambridge University Press, 2003), chapter 9.

state to the next and such chronological models may not be the most appropriate means to examine the subject.

Using Britain as a case study, it is clear that notions of consumer citizenship existed in the same period that Cohen describes. Peter Gurney has argued that the consumers' cooperative movement offered a coherent politics of consumption which acted as a real and viable alternative for many citizens in the late-nineteenth and early-twentieth centuries.[11] Frank Trentmann has taken the point further and suggested that co-operative commitment to free trade offered a vision of civil society beyond the state in which both collective and individual interests were served.[12] And, writing of the 1940s, Ina Zweiniger-Bargielowska has demonstrated the central role citizen housewives played in the administration of price controls and austerity measures during and after the war. She goes on to argue that Conservative Party appeals to these women consumers were a crucial factor in the final defeat of the Labour Government in 1951.[13]

While less work has appeared on the history of consumer politics since the 1950s, it is quite clear that material circumstances have played a dominant role at all times. Apart from cultural institutions that aimed to raise standards of taste or to oppose certain forms of consumption, the vast majority of consumer organisations in the first half of the twentieth century were concerned with prices, with issues of poverty and the rights to basic necessities. In contrast, increased affluence from the 1950s gave rise to a number of new consumer concerns, often centred around value for money, quality and access to the cheap mass-produced commodities that Cohen shows to have filled the

---

[11] P. Gurney, *Co-operative Culture and the Politics of Consumption in England, c. 1870-1930* (Manchester: Manchester University Press, 1996).
[12] F. Trentmann, 'Wealth versus welfare: The British Left between Free Trade and national political economy before the First World War', in *Historical Research*, 70:171, 1997, pp. 70-98; F. Trentmann, 'National identity and consumer politics', in D. Winch and P. O'Brien (eds), *The Political Economy of British Historical Experience, 1688-1914* (Oxford: Oxford University Press, 2002), pp. 215-242. F. Trentmann, 'Bread, milk and democracy: Consumption and citizenship in twentieth-century Britain', in Daunton and Hilton, *Politics of Consumption*, pp. 129-163.
[13] I. Zweiniger-Bargielowska, *Austerity in Britain: Rationing, Controls and Consumption, 1939-1955* (Oxford: Oxford University Press, 2000).

homes of suburban America. This basic division between the types of goods that have been the concern of consumer politics does not deny the importance of differing political traditions, but the material conditions within which consumer politics have been articulated are crucial. With this division between necessity and affluence, then, one has to be careful not to overlay it with an assumption of a close relationship between citizenship and consumption in the early period and an increasing separation between the two in the latter. Rather, just as Cohen argues, the citizen and consumer were 'ever-shifting categories that sometimes overlapped.'[14] But this negotiation between the two has continued from necessity to affluence and, in Britain at least, dynamic relationships have existed between consumption and citizenship well beyond the 1950s and, unlike Cohen's America, continue to do so today.

In Britain, ideas about citizenship and a politics of necessitous consumption first culminated in the First World War Consumers' Council.[15] Responding to widespread anger about food shortages, rising prices and profiteering, the government established a Ministry of Food and appointed a Food Controller, Lord Rhondda. He was advised by the Consumers' Council, appointed to represent the views and interests of ordinary working-class consumers, and which drew on several branches of the labour movement such as the Standing Joint Committee of Industrial Women's Organisations, the War Emergency: Workers' National Committee and the Co-operative movement. The Council was a measure of political containment, designed to appease the grievances of ordinary consumers who had elsewhere taken to the streets and who, the government was warned, might do so in Britain. Nevertheless, it was able to influence some aspects of state food control and became the focus for the development of a radical consumerism, urging the regulation of industry to end the practices of adulteration, under-weight selling and price-fixing which daily plagued the working-class consumer. The Council demonstrated the extent to

---

[14] Cohen, *Consumers' Republic*, p. 8.
[15] The following few paragraphs are a summary version of my *Consumerism in Twentieth-Century Britain: The Search for a Historical Movement* (Cambridge: Cambridge University Press, 2003).

which working-class politics was as much influenced by prices as wages. It formed an important precedent for consumer politics which were maintained throughout the interwar years, leading to the establishment of the Food Council in 1925, several cost-of-living campaigns organised by working-class women, and the demands of the Labour Party for an effective Consumers' Council in the 1930s with powers to enforce maximum prices. Here, trade union interests predominated over consumer concerns but beyond the Labour Party leadership consumerist thought flourished. The Independent Labour Party advocated the introduction of a 'living wage' policy, strongly influenced by the under-consumption theories of J. A. Hobson, the Co-operative movement continued to propagate its march to the 'co-operative commonwealth' and sympathisers such as Beatrice Webb, G. D. H. Cole and Percy Redfern attempted to marry co-operation's consumer power with the interests of workers and the state direction of industry.

Following its electoral success at the end of the Second World War, Labour was again provided with the opportunity to institutionalise the consumer as citizen. However, the consumer consultative machinery established within the newly nationalised industries was weak and ineffective, suggesting the greater willingness of Labour to listen to workers rather than consumers despite its manifesto commitments to 'fair shares' in its austerity measures. Once re-elected in 1950, though, the Labour government did launch a major investigation into the desirability of creating a state-sponsored Consumer Advisory Centre with the ability to influence prices and engage in the comparative testing of branded goods as the economy geared up towards the proliferation of new consumables in a period of reconstruction and promised affluence. Budgetary constraints and immediate political pressures soon put a stop to the scheme, as well as defeat in 1951, but the move did represent Labour's response to a growing concern with both affluent and necessitous goods from bodies as diverse as the trade unions and the think-tank Political and Economic Planning.

By this time, however, the politics of consumption was coming to be represented within official bodies less by the working-class female co-operator and more by the middle-class, non-feminist members of the National Council of Women.[16] In the 1950s it was these women who built upon their wartime consumer representational experiences to form the Women's Advisory Council (WAC) of the British Standards Institute. They advocated a consumerism based not upon transforming the organisation of the economy and the price mechanism, but upon the education of the individual, providing advice on wise shopping and how to claim redress and assistance. This was a consumerism that operated as a handmaiden to industry and was supported by many in government and business organisations. It was further promoted by the WAC's successor, the Consumer Advisory Council (CAC, 1955), the Conservative-appointed Molony Committee on Consumer Protection (1959-1962) and ultimately the Consumer Council (1963-1970) which continued to focus on education and information while having no power whatsoever to intervene in the marketplace or chase up individual grievances. It was an individualised, prochoice consumerism that would confirm the historical models developed for the post-war United States.

Nevertheless, such institutions, not yet examined in as great a depth in post-war American history, did act as rallying points for a burgeoning consumer movement. When the Conservatives abolished the Consumer Council in 1970, a general outcry was voiced by the press and the Conservatives were forced to respond, creating the Office of Fair Trading in 1973 which has remained a more effective watchdog on market abuses. The Council must also be seen as just one of a number of organisations committed to defending the consumer interest which has taken consumer politics well beyond the purely economic realm and into wider social questions of citizenship. Most importantly, the comparative testing body, the Consumers' Association (CA), set up in 1956 and modelled on the US Consumers Union, has been an important influence on UK legislation, such that one *Times* commentator was able to claim that by 1980 the CA had 'filled more pages of the statute book than any other pres-

---

[16] M. Hilton, 'The female consumer and the politics of consumption in twentieth-century Britain', in *Historical Journal*, 45:1, 2002, pp. 103-128.

sure group this century.'[17] The CA's main focus has been on obtaining better value for money for its subscribers to *Which?* magazine, and is thus open to the charge that it has fostered acquisitive individualism, but it has also been at the forefront of a more social, as opposed to economic, form of consumer politics. Its founders and organising council came mainly, if not entirely, from the social democratic wing of the Labour Party who saw in consumerism the potential for providing a middle way between the organised interests of business and trade unions. Some viewed consumerism as a new social movement and actively encouraged the proliferation of local consumer groups in the 1960s while others went on to work for the National Consumer Council (NCC), a government-funded body set up in 1975 which explicitly linked consumer politics to issues of citizenship rather than self-interest. The NCC's initial objective was to fight for the 'poor and disadvantaged' consumer, a goal which, if not so much the primary focus during the wider market reforms of the 1980s and 1990s, has at least in recent years come to the fore again.

Although this has been only a cursory overview, it does point to the continuing interplay between citizenship and consumption in the period Cohen argues was merely 'consumerised'. One could cite also the rise of ethical and green consumerism, the concern with low-income consumers by bodies such as the Child Poverty Action Group, and the continued attention to the consumer-voter in party-political discourse. Indeed, it is in government rhetoric about consumers that we can see some of the prevailing ambivalence about the relationship between the citizen and the consumer. Following initiatives such as John Major's *Citizen's Charter* (1991), Tony Blair, in *Modern Markets: Confident Consumers* (1999), promised to put 'consumers centre-stage' and 'ensure that consumers' concerns are heard in Government.'[18] Significantly, though, the document refuses to define the consumer interest at any point and threatens both to reduce consumerism to the lowest common denominator of dependence on 'wealth generated by business' and enable the consumer interest to be articulated by

---

[17] Cited in Consumers' Association (CA), in *Annual Report, 1979-1980* (London: CA, 1980), p. 13.
[18] Department of Trade and Industry, *Modern Markets: Confident Consumers*, Cm 4410 (London: HMSO, 1999), p. 6.

groups other than consumers. Yet it must also be seen as part of a continuing process of liaison and negotiation that does provide substantial opportunities for input from the consumer movement. Its concerns must also be analysed in the context of other government initiatives demonstrating a revitalised consumer citizenship debate. The NCC is constantly seeking new means of increasing consumer participation and representation and it continues to work not only to educate consumers and regulate markets in the consumer interest, but also to tackle issues of exclusion for those on low incomes, and develop consumer protection measures as and when the need arises.[19] Its working principles are still based around access, choice, safety, information, redress, representation and fairness (what was formally termed 'equity') and many of its main policy issues remain the same: the relationship between the consumer and the citizen; the definition of the consumer interest; the constituency of the NCC as a representative body; and the ability to maintain an independent voice.[20]

In other countries, differing and continuing relationships between citizenship and consumption can also be observed. In Sweden, activity in consumer affairs in the 1940s and 1950s by trade unions, co-operatives, voluntary and women's organisations was later taken up by the state (i.e. the Statens Konsumentråd). Later still, Sweden established the world's first consumer ombudsman as well as a Market Court in 1971 and, in 1973, the state-sponsored National Board for Consumer Policies (Konsumentverket, merging with the ombudsman in 1976). With such top-down consumer protection, no national federation of independent consumer groups was thought necessary until the Co-operative Union established a Consumer Policy Council to serve as a forum for the co-operative, labour and consumer movements (becoming the Consumer Council in 1992). In Sweden, then, the role of the state has been particularly strong, though it has worked closely in combination with a range of consumer voluntary associations, offering a very different type of consumer conscious-

---

[19] National Consumer Council (NCC), *Involving Consumers: Everyone Benefits* (London: NCC, 2002).
[20] NCC, *What is the National Consumer Council?* (London: NCC, 2002); private correspondence between author and Anna Bradley, NCC Director, 8 January 2002.

ness than the private mass comparative-testing organisation of the UK.[21] In France, as in Sweden, there existed strong traditions of co-operative activity and ideas through the works of Charles Gide (and Anders Örne in Sweden) in the early-twentieth century.[22] In the shift to post-Second World War affluence, the Union fédérale de la consommation (UFC) and its publication, *Que Choisir*, represented the comparative testing tradition, but consumerism reflected also the concerns of family voluntary organisations, rural groups and the older traditions of the labour and co-operative movement. All these entered into a dialogue with the state through the 1960 National Committee of Consumers, though the government-funded, yet independent, Institut National de la Consommation (INC, the publishers of *50 million de consommateurs*) has provided the main institutional focus for consumerism and has subsequently promoted several instances of protection legislation as well as the greater codification of consumer law within the *Code civil*.[23] While the UFC has therefore promoted a seemingly typical market-oriented comparative testing type of consumerism, it has had to compete with several other consumer voices that have often advocated a more radical, if not always more influential, type of consumerism.[24]

In Germany, radical consumer politics were manifested in the earlier period through consumers' leagues, co-operative societies and the actions of protesting women on the streets of Berlin at the end of the First World War.[25] Even under the Nazi regime, attention was given to consumption and material possessions and the female consumer was mobilised, if

---

[21] K. Blomqvist, 'Swedish consumer movement', in Brobeck et al., *Encyclopaedia*, pp. 544-547; Consumers International, *Balancing the Scales, Part 1: Consumer Protection in Sweden and the United Kingdom* (London: Consumers International, 1995).
[22] E. Furlough, *Consumer Co-operation in France: The Politics of Consumption, 1834-1930* (Ithaca: Cornell University Press, 1991).
[23] L. Bihl, *Consommateur: Défends-toi!* (Paris: Denoël, 1976).
[24] G. Trumbull, 'Strategies of consumer group mobilisation: France and Germany in the 1970s', in Daunton and Hilton, *Politics of Consumption*, pp. 261-282; A. Morin, 'French consumer movement', in Brobeck et al., *Encyclopaedia*, pp. 279-283.
[25] W. Breckman, 'Disciplining consumption: The debate on luxury in Wilhelmine Germany, 1890-1914', in *Journal of Social History*, 24 (1991), pp. 485-505; B. J. Davis, *Home Fires Burning: Food, Politics and Everyday Life in World War I Berlin* (Chapel Hill: University of North Carolina Press, 2000).

in a highly circumscribed manner, for propaganda initiatives.[26] In the transition to affluence, a comparative-testing organisation, Stiftung Warentest, was created in 1964, though, in contrast to other western consumer organisations, the impetus came from the labour movement and, mainly, the government. This close relationship with the state, which continues to subsidise its activities, has also meant that German consumerism has maintained closer links with business and direct access to government decision-making. Outside of Berlin, Verbraucher-Zentrale (consumer centres) have also been established in each of the regional states and close collaboration has existed between these and voluntary consumer bodies through the Arbeitsgemeinschaft der Verbraucherbände, established as early as 1953. All this has resulted in a consumerism less radical than in France but a perhaps more influential one in which consumers have been more closely incorporated within state institutions.[27]

Beyond affluent Europe, consumerism has provided further political models. In pre-war Japan, consumer politics was limited to a small co-operative movement. The term 'consumption' suffered negative connotations and individuals were in any case encouraged to save rather then consume in order to finance economic expansion and industrialisation. Citizens in the post-war period have, by contrast, embraced their roles as consumers, although they have often come into confrontation with a pro-business state. Nevertheless, Japanese consumers have maintained a citizen consumer model based upon the wider national interest, often sacrificing cheapness and choice for other social and economic goals, be it agricultural protectionism or the quality of life.[28] In Southeast Asia, since 1965, comparative-testing consumerism has

---

[26] N. Reagin, 'Comparing apples and oranges: Housewives and the politics of consumption in interwar Germany', in Strasser et al., *Getting and Spending*, pp. 241-262; H. Berghoff, 'Enticement and deprivation: The regulation of consumption in pre-war Nazi Germany', in Daunton and Hilton, *Politics of Consumption*, pp. 165-184.
[27] E. Kuhlmann, 'German consumer movement', in Brobeck et al., *Encyclopaedia*, pp. 289-293.
[28] P. L. Maclachlan, *Consumer Politics in Postwar Japan: The Institutional Boundaries of Citizen Activism* (New York: Columbia University Press, 2002); M. Imai, 'Japanese consumer movement', in Brobeck et al., *Encyclopaedia*, pp. 341-342.

emerged as an influential movement, especially in Malaysia. Although many of its consumer organisations reflected the affluence of one section of its population (e.g. in the Federal Territory Consumers' Association), Malaysian consumers have subsequently played a prominent role in changing the direction of global consumerism more generally. In 1960, several European private testing organisations joined with the American Consumers Union to found the International Organisation of Consumers Unions (IOCU, now Consumers International) designed to 'act as a clearing house for information on test programmes'.[29] Immediately, however, it went beyond this, first taking on board the agendas of the state-assisted consumer councils of the Scandinavian countries and, from the 1970s, the interests of developing-world consumers, concerned less with value for money and more with the right to enjoy a basic standard of living. Malaysian consumers have played a prominent role in this development, not least because of the creation of an IOCU Regional Office for Asia and the Pacific (CI-ROAP) in Kuala Lumpur in 1974.[30]

It is in these trans-national developments that we can see new developments in citizen-consumer models being fought out at an international level. Indeed, within a global economic system, it should come as no surprise that consumerism has shifted its terrain from separate national contexts to take into account the diverse interests of consumers across the world. In Europe, consumer organisations have come together in bodies such as the Bureau Européen des Unions de Consommateurs (BEUC) which helped play a role in setting down the five 'fundamental rights' of the consumer by the European Council in 1975, as well as the first programme for a Consumer Protection and Information Policy, agreed upon by the Council of Ministers.[31] Similarly, the IOCU has pushed

---

[29] F. G. Sim, *IOCU on Record: A Documentary History of the International Organisation of Consumers Unions, 1960-1990* (New York: Consumers Union, 1991), p. 27.
[30] J. Fernandez, 'Asian-Pacific consumer movement', in Brobeck et al., *Encyclopaedia*, pp. 38-41.
[31] H. W. Micklitz and S. Weatherill, 'Consumer policy in the European Community: Before and after Maastricht', *Journal of Consumer Policy*, 16:3-4, 1993, pp. 285-322; European Commission, *European Consumer Guide to the Single Market* (Brussels: Office of Official Publications of the European Communities, 1994).

for the establishment of consumer rights within the United Nations, where it has achieved Category I status, enabling it to speak as a national delegation (though it cannot vote). The UN has focused on topics such as unethical marketing (for example, Nestlé's infant milk formula) and product safety, resulting in the publication, from 1982, of a *UN Consolidated List of Banned Products*. In 1985, it also established a set of Guidelines for Consumer Protection which has acted as an important reference for the development of consumer protection legislation in Asian, African and South American states.[32] The Guidelines have thus ensured that the principles of organised western consumerism have provided the models for the development of nation-specific politics of consumption elsewhere, but they also make reference to food and other essential goods and services, reflecting the politics of necessitous consumption which is still most relevant to the majority of nations. By the mid-1990s, the UN Commission for Sustainable Development and the UN Economic and Social Council were urging the inclusion of guidelines on the promotion of sustainable consumption, placing duties as well as rights on consumers to think further than the boundaries of rational self-interest contained within the comparative-testing model.[33]

All this is not to deny the obvious trends within a neoliberal marketplace to reduce the consumer to the individual shopper or the utility-maximising individual, but it is to emphasise that the debate as to the relationship between consumption and citizenship is far from over. The IOCU has expanded rapidly over the last few decades such that there are now over 250 affiliated institutions from well over 100 states. It has become increasingly dominated by the concerns of the developing world, and its expressed basic consumer rights (which include the rights to a healthy environment and to basic needs) invoke more the duties of consumers, in a manner similar to late-nineteenth and early-twentieth century activists, than the assumed actions of self-interest some historians have ascribed to late-twentieth century consumer

---

[32] United Nations, *Guidelines for Consumer Protection* (New York 1986); D. Harland, 'The United Nations Guidelines for Consumer Protection', in *Journal of Consumer Policy*, 10 (1987), 245-266.
[33] A. Peterson and J. M. Halloran, 'United Nations Consumer Protections', in Brobeck et al., *Encyclopaedia*, pp. 581-583.

groups. Ultimately, the financing of the IOCU campaigns, many of which are indistinguishable from the demands of the anti-globalisation movement, comes from the pockets of subscribers to *Which?*, *Consumer Reports*, *Que Choisir* and *Test*, those very same publications that have been so readily dismissed as organs of acquisitive individualism. It is no doubt likely that the vast majority of organised consumers are unaware of how their money is spent, but it is nevertheless still relevant to speak of consumers as citizens especially as global consumer politics continue to spread into the developing world and the former Soviet bloc, at all times taking into account the concerns of new citizens and new publics.

What this suggests for the future study of consumer politics (and much profitable research could be extended into all of the case studies mentioned above) is that, outside the United States at least, consumerism has not become impoverished over the last two or three decades. Instead, different models are perhaps necessary. Firstly, the distinction between necessity and affluence is crucial to understanding the chronological difference between two broad types of consumer politics. The material circumstances, whether poverty or affluence, within which consumers have found themselves in Britain, the United States, France, Germany and Sweden have had important influences on the types of consumer-citizen ideals developed. However, it is clear that the development of consumer politics in these countries has also been characterised by strong links between the interests of the poor and of the affluent. Secondly, though, what is also apparent is that how the politics of necessity and of affluence have manifested themselves has relied on the different national political cultures of individual states and consumer movements. The relationship between citizens and consumers, state and individuals, associations and civil society have differed in significant ways from one country to the next.

And thirdly, as consumerism has expanded beyond the affluent West, it has again taken on board the concerns of poorer consumers, so that affluence is being recombined with necessity within a social justice model of consumer politics. Better information available to western consumers in the global information society, together with the rise of single-issue politics and various forms of campaigning networks, have meant that new forms of consumer citizenship are emerging on a world political stage. This is not simply a matter of the growing popularity of fair trade organisations and goods, and the expansion of almost philanthropic ethical consumer initiatives, in which Western consumers mobilise their duties to fellow citizens: it is also about the forms of dialogue that have emerged between rich and poor consumers within various organisational contexts and in the attempts to incorporate the consumer interest within global economic, social and political institutions, from the World Trade Organisation to the UN. This is a development that no one can yet offer a definitive interpretation of, since it is a story still very much being played out in the policy arena, but it does at least demonstrate that citizens have not been entirely 'consumerised' in the sense Cohen speaks of in the America of the 1980s and 1990s. It recognises that the relationship between, and the history of, consumption and citizenship is by no means over and that it is far too premature to end a history of consumer politics in such a negative manner.

III

'Free choice lies at the core of our economic system': A comparative history of post-war British and American consumer organisations.

Lawrence Black

If the expansion of National Trust membership, making it Europe's largest voluntary organisation, signals the potency of ideas about national heritage in post-war Britain, then it hardly strains the bounds of interpretation to see in the largest *new* voluntary association of this same period, the Consumers' Association (CA), evidence of a burgeoning consumer society. Britons were ever more a nation of shoppers in circumstances of choice more than necessity. In Jennifer Jenkins (who chaired the National Trust 1986-90 and the CA 1965-76) these developments were conjoined.[1] Whether related to the liberation of self-expression in 'the 1960s', economic individualism or, conversely, to resistance to global capitalism, the growth of consumer testing organisations marked the politics of the shop floor and the domestic. If key as Britain's imperial horizons receded, these also figured in

---

A version of this paper was presented to the Royal Historical Society / NACBS Conference, *Crosstown Traffic: Anglo-American Cultural Exchange since 1865*, Warwick University, 2004.

[1] 'The National Trust and National Heritage', in D. Cannadine, *In Churchill's Shadow* (London: Penguin, 2003). R. Hewison, *The Heritage Industry* (London: Methuen, 1987). On CA, L. Black, 'Which?craft in Post-War Britain: The Consumers' Association and the politics of affluence', in *Albion* 36:1 (2004).

Cold War confrontations like the Khrushchev-Nixon 'Kitchen Debate'. Consumerists' concern with everyday durables helped define post-war affluence in domestic, individualist terms. Behind such mundane agendas lay a host of broader visions, radical sensibilities (most apparent in consumer campaigner Ralph Nader, 'the world's toughest customer'), legislative initiatives and ways of marshalling both the politics of consumption and consuming as a political act.[2]

Parallels or the US founding fathers show Which? way to turn

If the growth of testing organisations in developed liberal democracies evinced growing material abundance, it also suggested western Europe was emulating American social patterns. Consumers Union (CU) was formed in 1936 (its forerunner Consumer's Research in 1929). European organisations grew as either state-funded products of World War Two or independently as affluence set in during the 1950s. It was only post-war that CU established a sizeable membership. Having contracted in the war, it vaulted from 55,000 in 1945 to 700,000 by 1954 and 1.25 million by 1967, expanding in tandem with shopping malls (numbering 8 in 1945 and 3,840 by 1960) and advertising volume (its chosen index).[3]

CU influenced European developments. Esther Peterson, a CU board member and wife of the Labor Attaché at the US embassy in Stockholm, alerted Colston Warne (CU's President until 1979) to the Swedish state-sponsored consumer organisations. Warne attended a 1956 Commons meeting that led to the CA's founding. Dorothy Goodman, a US student living in London, is credited with the first inkling of a British version of CU's *Consumer Reports* and later became an associate editor of

---

[2] 'The World's Toughest Customer', *Time*, 12th December 1969. See M. Hilton, *Consumerism in Twentieth-Century Britain* (Cambridge: Cambridge University Press, 2003); L. Cohen, *A Consumers' Republic: The politics of mass consumption in post-war America* (New York: Knopf, 2002).
[3] 'Judgement at Mount Vernon', in *Sales Management*, 2nd April 1965; 'CU puts on Muscle', in *Business Week*, 23rd December 1967; 'Consumers Union: Feeding advice to hungry customers', in *Business Week*, 20th March 1954. L. Glickman (ed.), *Consumer Society in American History* (Ithaca: Cornell University Press, 1999), p. 5.

Consumer Reports. An ex-student of Warne's in the Paris Marshall Plan office helped establish a Danish product-testing lab. CU provided monies to start up the CA (which in turn lent it to the Belgian Association des Consommateurs) and the International Organisation of Consumer Unions (IOCU) in 1960.[4]

The CA and CU were non-profit organisations and spawned local consumer groups. Neither took advertising for fear of undermining the legitimacy of their tests of consumer durables and services, and threatened legal action against advertisers using its reports. CU boasted it had never lost a case and the CA lost only one in the 1960s. Equally, both were skilled at the hard sell of themselves. The CA borrowed testing initiatives from CU, notably contraceptives, drugs and sundry remedies. After expansion, both faced unfamiliar challenges in the 1970s. For CU (and Nader), Watergate raised the scandal stakes that consumerism had successfully dealt in. As the 'golden age' of economic growth was tarnished, their value to consumers in harder times was tested. In 1974 the CA explained that it was 'no more immune than individual consumers... from the ravages of inflation' and had launched *Holiday Which?* into 'the most serious recession in the travel trade since the war.' It justified a hike in subscriptions (the source of 80 percent of its income) arguing that 'in difficult and unsettled times there is surely added value in a service that saves consumers money, worry and disappointment.'[5]

Common to both were members who were a 'consumer aristocracy', 'the cream of the durable goods market' as CU dubbed them. Class trumped gender in consumerists' thinking, although their audience (particularly CA's) turned out to be more male than imagined. In 1962, Gallup reckoned CA members were three times more likely than Britons as a whole to be middle class. Of CU's 1954 members, 8.5 percent were in labour unions, but 43.5 percent were professionals. As one CU subscriber told *Esquire*, 'It doesn't strike me that Joe Milkman reads *CR* and of course, he's the one who should.' Whilst revelling in their members' purchasing power and educated, discriminating reputation, neither was solely or originally wooing this audience. CU had targeted workers

---

[4] Eirlys Roberts, *IOCU, 1960-80* (London: CA/IOCU, 1981), pp. 3, 10.
[5] 'Judgement at Mount Vernon'. CA, in *Annual Report* (1974), pp. 6-7.

in the depression and the CA strove to appeal to workers, whom it feared lacked the experience to rationally dispose of their new income in affluent Britain.[6] Both reconciled themselves with the belief that consumers were exploited by abundance no less than they suffered during shortages.

Still, difficulties reaching beyond this comparatively privileged audience had a moderating effect. In 1954 *Business Week* noted that CU's 'early crusading zeal has faded' and it increasingly pandered to middlebrow markets (or 'no longer tells its readers to clean their teeth with salt'). Both received approval from politics' commanding heights. President Kennedy's 1962 Consumer Message to Congress feted CU with a 'significant role in expanding the horizons of an informed public.' Prime Minister Wilson sent the CA tenth anniversary greetings in 1967.[7]

The CA's instigator Michael Young detected in such plaudits that CA was too 'accepted and respectable'. In a 1969 speech, Warne counselled CU, 'Don't unconsciously fall victim to love of ease and of approval.'[8] Success and affluence seemed to detract from the founding idealism. Nader said on leaving CU's board in 1974 that he considered CU 'a sleeping giant', but added, 'I wish higher-ups in the organisation would stop doing things like drinking Coke and eating hot dogs... it's very upsetting.'[9] These tensions were apparent in *Consumer Reports* and *Which?* 'Clinical muckraking', 'laconic', 'blunt', 'contemptuous', 'anti-glitter' was how *Sales Management* depicted *Consumer Reports*. *Which?* spoke with clarity, unimpressed by marketing fuss or whims of taste, but admiring the self-control subsistence enforced (and abundance threatened). There was a spartan air to consum-

---

[6] 'Judgement at Mount Vernon', in Gallup, *Enquiry into Which?* (1962), p. 3b, CA Archives, London Box A31 (CAA A31); 'Feeding advice', *Consumer Reports* (April 1962).
[7] ' Feeding advice', in *Consumer Reports* (April 1962), p. 165; *Which?* (October 1967), pp. 292-293.
[8] 'Proceedings of Consumer Assembly' (1967), pp. 22-23. CAA A67. 'Carrying the economics of dissent into effective action', Thomas M. Brooks Papers Box 2 File 3 (Brooks 2/3) Consumers' Movement Archive, Hale Library, Kansas State University (KSU), Manhattan, KS. He added, 'Don't be bitter, a sense of humor wins arguments.'
[9] '*Consumer Reports* knows what's best for us all', *Esquire*, February 1974, pp. 144-148.

erism: CU's origins in the depression informed its understanding of 'wise-spending', likewise the CA's genesis in post-war austerity. Nader's puritan work ethic was regularly noted; discouraging co-workers from drinking, but expecting them to dress respectably and cut their hair.[10]

This put them at odds with an ethos of conspicuous consumption. The CA and CU were ill-disposed to articulate style, fashion or beauty just as affluence afforded greater emphasis on it. Design issues seemed commensurate with the 'annual model racket' or contrived obsolescence. As Mckellar shows, CU remained wedded to functional consumption, but was enticed away by the tastes of its auto-driving, gadget-loving, suburban readers. What also put CU on the defensive was that affluence meant the 'moral claim' to represent the general good now lay with business and the consumers' republic' (with spending not thrift as the economy's dynamic, a patriotic duty), rather than with the consumer protection movement as in the 1930s. In Cohen's estimation, by the late 1950s *Consumer Reports* was a 'buying guide to consumer durables for a more and more affluent, educated, professional middle-class.'[11] The CA encouraged utility based decision-making. 'We can say that an electric iron is safe or a refrigerator efficient because we have tested it', *Which?* explained, 'We cannot say that the iron looks good or that the refrigerator looks ugly.' [12] But it too was lured by its audience's preferences; cars, overseas holidays, even au pairs. Its thrifty advice was used by those who could best afford it. They benefited from it more (as the middle classes did from the welfare state) than those it felt most needed the advice.

French, West German and Scandinavian organisations were state funded, but the CA and CU were voluntary associations. The *Harvard Business Review* felt this marked 'free enterprise at work, on the consumer side' and the 'decline of demand in recent years for greater government supervision.' More than the Cold War US context, dissatisfaction with the

---

[10]'Judgement at Mount Vernon'; 'Nader: Shining knight or a plotter?', in *Chicago Daily News* 16th November 1971.
[11] Susie McKellar, '"The Beauty of Stark Utility": Rational consumption in America – *Consumer Reports* 1936-54', in Judy Attfield (ed.), *Utility Reassessed: The Role of Ethics in the Practice of Design* (Manchester: Manchester University Press, 1999); Cohen, *Consumers' Republic*, pp. 130-131.
[12]*Which?* (July 1959), p. 63.

bureaucracy of the Attlee government's nationalised industry consumer boards and the traditional voluntarist instincts of UK social policy inspired the CA. As long-standing council member John Thirlwell saw it, the CA 'swamp[ed] all the efforts of [the] state to create poodles to represent consumers.' But the CA also promoted intervention, pushing for the state Consumer Council (CC) from 1963 and encouraging legislation like 1968's Trades Descriptions Act. It needed the state to reach less privileged consumers as the National Consumer Council did from 1975, directed by Young, then Jeremy Mitchell and Maurice Healy, all of whom 'learned their basic consumerism at CA.' *The Times* reckoned that by 1980 the CA had 'filled more pages of the statute book than any other pressure group this century.'[13]

Nader influenced legislation in the 1960s (on cars, gas pipelines, meat, workplace safety and the 1968 Radiation Control Act) and the reorganisation of the Federal Drug Administration and Trade Commission. CU's long-standing demands were also met via the Truth-in-Packaging Bill (1966) and Truth-in-Lending Bill (1968). CU, like the CA, provided personnel for federal schemes, such as Esther Peterson, who became President Johnson's Special Assistant for Consumer Affairs in 1964 and later served under Jimmy Carter.[14]

Historians have rightly emphasised American influence on the IOCU and CA. But in other ways – not least considering the institutional culture of consumerists besides ideology, as attempted here – the process was more one of adapting than adopting an American model and illustrates differences of national and political cultures as much as parallels.[15] Young reported of his 1958 trip to CU's Mount

---

[13] Eugene R. Beem, John S.Ewing, 'Business appraises consumer testing agencies', in *Harvard Business Review* (March-April 1954). J.Thirlwell, 'An overview of the Consumer Movement in Britain', 26th March 1989, Thirlwell Box, KSU. *Times* 10th April 1980
[14] R. O.Hermann, 'The Consumer Movement in Perspective' (n.d. c.1971), pp. 18-28. Brooks 1/12.
[15] Early comparisons feature in J. Martin and G.W. Smith, *The Consumer Interest* (London: Pall Mall Press, 1968), ch. 15. See M. Hilton, 'Americanisation, British Consumerism and the International Organisation of Consumers Unions' in M. Kipping, N. Tiratsoo (eds), *Americanisation in 20th Century Europe: Business, Culture, Politics* (Lille: Université Charles-de-Gaulle, 2001); C. Beauchamp, 'Getting *Your Money's Worth*: American models for the re-making

Vernon HQ, that 'CU has very few impressive people, except for Dexter Masters, but the set-up is very impressive.'[16] The CA (like many British politicians) thought it could show Americans how to do things better. And like popular music in the 1960s (if not politics), they did. The CA broke CU-based membership projections of a ¼ million membership ceiling by the end of 1959 and more than doubled it by 1969 (and the CA's membership density was topped by the Dutch Consumentenbond).[17]

There was then irony in the CA's silver jubilee gift to CU in 1961: a map of IOCU affiliates and inscribed, 'Greetings to the founding father from the pilgrims in London who would not have known *Which?* way to turn.'[18] The Atlantic was regularly traversed. In 1958 Casper Brook (the CA's soon-to-be-director) and Consumentenbond's Elizabeth Schadee sounded out CU on financial help for their groups and an international organisation. Jim Northcott was the earliest Briton to visit in 1952. Northcott worked with Brook in *The Economist*'s Intelligence Unit on return and helped found the CA. His 1953 Fabian pamphlet *Value for Money?* argued that stricter English libel laws made a private consumer advisory service unlikely. Northcott was further persuaded that a public organisation was more likely to succeed because it had to reach beyond 'the richer and better educated consumers, that is, those least in need of its help', currently attracted to CU and who he hazarded were most likely to be drawn to a British equivalent. Northcott mined *Consumer Reports*' uproarious findings and mimicked its irreverent style, noting the product advertised as ending the need for lawn mowing which killed grass and the 'kiss-proof' lipstick that was anything but.[19]

---

of the Consumer interest in Britain, 1930s-1960s', in M. Bevir, F. Trentmann (eds), *Critiques of Capital in Modern Britain and America* (Basingstoke: Palgrave, 2002) and P. Maclachlan and F. Trentmann, 'Civilising markets: Traditions of consumer politics in twentieth-century Britain, Japan and the United States', in M. Bevir, F. Trentmann (eds), *Markets in Historical Contexts* (Cambridge: Cambridge University Press, 2004).
[16] Note of Informal Meeting, Mary Adams' House, 20th January 1959, CA council minutes.
[17] C. Brook, 'The Discriminating Consumer' (1959), p.15, CAA A27. CA, in *Annual Report* (1969), pp. 4, 11.
[18] CU, *This is Consumers' Union* (New York: CU, 1961), Brooks 2/16.
[19] Roberts, *IOCU*, p.3. Interview, Northcott, 14th February 2001. J. F. Northcott, *Value for Money? The Case for a Consumers' Advice Service* (London: Fabian Society, 1953), pp. 3-12.

'Promoting skepticism'

This was satire, a very 1960s mode, though that the CA imported this ironic critique from the USA confounds certain cultural assumptions about ironic character and appreciation. It had long been present, apparent in Chase and Schlink's *Your Money's Worth* (1927), a founding text of the US consumer movement. The CA and CU saw themselves supplying product information that advertising and branding was not. As full employment, pay, the range of goods and self-service shopping grew in the 1950s, such information was priceless to make good notions of freedom of choice or consumer sovereignty. As Warne put it in 1961, 'For many years it was customary for... manufacturers to proclaim the consumer "king" and to say they had to dance to the consumer's tune. But the opposite was much more... the actual situation.' Instead of aiding consumers, Warne told the Advertising Federation of America, 'not insubstantial segments of your industry embarked upon a program of superlatives, half-truths, pseudo-science and irrelevancies which, inadequately policed in your own ranks or by federal authority, brought us to your doorstep.'[20]

CU believed that 'Advertising is a valid mechanism for the dissemination of information', but 'may be used to communicate truth or fallacy.' Presently it was used to sell and complement goods, not inform. Warne felt advertising's 'chief threat... lies in the tendency to appeal to irrational motivations.'[21] 'Uninformed choice is not free', he explained, 'you cannot boast of a vote of confidence [in a product] when the voter has been denied the knowledge essential to rational choice.' Morris Kaplan, CU's technical director, told *Sales Management* he saw CU as 'a promoter of skepticism... opposed to the establishment which would have "freedom of choice" made simply on the basis of advertising claims.'[22]

---

[20] C.Warne, 'The Consumer, victim of planned obsolescence', City Club, Cleveland, 18th February 1961, p. 3; 'Economic and Social Aspects of Advertising', Advertising Federation of America, Washington, 29th May 1961, Brooks, 1/47. S. Chase, F.J. Schlink, *Your Money's Worth: A study in the waste of the consumer's dollar* (New York: Macmillan, 1927).
[21] *Atlanta Constitution* 3rd August 1969. *New York Times*, 1st April 1962.
[22] Warne, 'Economic and Social Aspects of Advertising'; 'Judgement at Mount Vernon'.

The market was a less potent language in Britain's mixed economy, but the CA felt business, government and advertisers were impeding the potential for consumer sovereignty. Like CU, the CA's growth correlated with that of advertising, notably on TV from 1955. *Which?* set itself as an antidote to advertisers' hocus-pocus. Consumerists like Tony Crosland, a CA council member until 1964, protested against Heath's abolition of the Consumer Council (CC) in 1970 on the grounds that, 'Competition will not work properly unless the consumer is well informed.'[23]

As business was accused of abusing consumers' trust, so they charged consumer organisations with fostering 'suspicion of business and government'. As General Motors (GM) Chairman James Roche saw it, CU and Nader aimed 'to alienate the American consumer from business, to tear down long-established relationships that have served both so well.' Sowing doubt in consumers' minds was an accusation hurled at CU since the 1930s.[24] The CA and CU riled business by deploying what it considered its language of free choice. Provoking opponents was the essence of Nader's method. The *National Observer* concluded in 1968 that *Consumer Reports* was 'read, respected and feared', for its ability to make or break a company. In 1971, its criticisms of STP's oil additive ('makes engines young again') wiped 20 percent off the company's Wall Street value. The *Harvard Business Review* was less certain CU wielded such power, especially over unknown brands. Schlink, whose Consumer's Research survived the 1936 schism, accused CU and Nader of a 'running fusillade against business' and wanting 'more things run by government'. The Federation of British Industry and Aims of Industry griped that the CA grilled the private more than the public sector. *Which?* sent 'cold shudders up and down the spine', of the retail journal, *The Grocer*.[25]

---

[23] Alma Williams, *Educating the Consumer* (London: Longman, 1975), p.16; *Focus*, September 1970, p. 14.
[24] *Fortune* (May 1971); Roche in 'shining knight or a plotter?'; McKellar, 'The Beauty of Stark Utility', p. 75.
[25] 'Sending marketplace scamps into economic tailspin, in *Holyoke Transcript-Telegram*, 19th July 1971; *National Observer*, 26th February 1968; *Which?* (Winter 1958), pp. 20-21.

Standard charges were that test methods were unscientific (and corrections were a regular *Which?* feature) and that they impeded enterprising initiatives by criticising innovations early in their development.[26] Others concluded CU was 'a highly competent, professional organisation, not a collection of gadflies.'[27] Gradually business began to mellow towards testing bodies. The advertisers' journal *Printer's Ink* admitted as early as 1940 that CU had made copywriters 'more careful in their claims'. Though it was still a novelty when supermarket chain owner David Sainsbury endorsed the CA, or US Chamber of Commerce President Edward Rust, to the consternation of the Chicago chamber, applauded Nader.[28]

CU's defence of free choice allowed it to simultaneously pose as pro-American values, anti-communist and the champion of everyday consumers' rights. It was a quintessentially New Deal entity, countervailing commercial power. But CU's $4.1 million income in 1964-1965 could hardly contest a $12 billion advertising industry. Perhaps irreverence was its best resource? The CA's vision, expressed in Young's *The Chipped White Cups of Dover*, was of discriminating consumer-citizens, improving production quality, breaking the grip of the pro-producer main political parties and the wage-price spiral and reversing national decline. *Which?* was as withering as CU towards advertising flannel, its tone imitated by (and precursory to) the 1962-1963 TV satire, *That Was The Week That Was*.[29] But damning verdicts on British cars led some to question its patriotism. 'So-called consumer associations devote their time to harsh criticism of British goods' that 'were gleefully seized upon by our foreign competitors',

---

[26] Elisabeth Houlton, *Which? Put to the Test* (Aims of Industry, 1967), p. 13; Ruby Turner Morris, *CU: Methods, Implications, Weaknesses and Strengths* (New London, Conn., 1971), pp. 54-56.
[27] Beem, Ewing, 'Business appraises consumer testing'. 'Implications of the existence of CU for marketers of major appliances and related Consumer Durables', (MBA, New York University, 1965), p. 31, Brooks 2/16.
[28] 'Feeding advice'; *Printer's Ink*, 28th June 1940; Sainsbury in P. Goldman, 'Consumerism, Art or Science?', in *Journal of the Royal Society of Arts* (August 1969). Rust, *Business Week*, 22nd September 1973, p. 31.
[29] M.Young, *The Chipped White Cups of Dover: A discussion of the possibility of a new progressive party* (London: Unit 2, 1960); B. Levin, *The Pendulum Years* (London: Cape, 1970), p. 321.

the *Daily Express* seethed. Neither the CA nor CU cared for campaigns of the 'buy British' sort.[30]

CU's irreverence, notwithstanding its claim to be *the* true believer in the market, could be represented as anti-capitalist or un-American, especially towards the iconic automobile and TV. Warne considered the social costs of TV to 'include the cost to each buyer of the Anacin to cure the headaches induced by the programming' and bemoaned how 'lunacy' had become 'the chief characteristic of car design', driving up fuel consumption and repair costs. Faith that the 'educated consumer will triumph' was hard to sustain whilst the present-day American was seen as 'a cultural doughnut with the rim knocked off.'[31]

Guinea Pigs and Affluent Sheep

'The weakening of the power of the consumer as a rationally motivated, well-informed arbiter to the marketplace threatens us', Dexter Masters, CU's director from 1958 explained. 'Withdraw consumer sovereignty and free competition becomes a kind of jungle warfare.'[32] Besides taming corporate beasts, an occasional upshot of this was a derogatory view of consumers. This language of the jungle was a recurrent theme, echoing Upton Sinclair's 1906 muckraking expose of meat-packing, *The Jungle*, but also imagining consumers as a herd, corralled by big business. Schlink and Kallett's classic, *100,000,000 Guinea Pigs* (1933) was 'so-called because American consumers were pictured as "guinea pigs" who offered themselves for experimental testing by purchasing all sorts of pernicious and doubtful products.'[33] *Which?* editor

---

[30] *Daily Express*, 12th April 1962. Dana Frank, *Buy American* (Boston: Beacon Press, 1999)
[31] C.Warne 'The economic impact of advertising', 4th February 1961; 'Planned obsolescence', p. 3; 'A consumer looks at leisure', May 1961, Brooks 1/47. A. Offer, in *The American Automobile Frenzy of the 1950s* (Oxford: Oxford Discussion Papers in Economic and Social History no. 11, 1996).
[32] Morris Kaplan, 'Caveat Emptor', 23rd April 1965, p. 3. Brooks 2/19.
[33] 'Taming the Corporate Tiger', in *The Ralph Nader Reader* (New York: Seven Stories Press, 2000); Beem, Ewing, 'Business appraises consumer testing', pp. 113-4. U. Sinclair, *The Jungle* (New York: Jungle Publishing Co., 1906) A. Kallett, F.J. Schlink, *100,000,000 Guinea Pigs* (New York: Vanguard Press, 1933).

Eirlys Roberts believed 'legal language is often used to bilk the underprivileged' and by 1980 that, 'Anyone who does not know what a consumer organisation is, now, must be... unconscious.' Northcott acquired a sense of the 'gullible American public'. Nader declared himself 'vexed by the isolation and apathy of the citizen.' Millar's *The Affluent Sheep*, commissioned by CA, but disowned when it castigated consumers' 'apathy, carelessness and irresponsibility', nonetheless confirmed the CA's opinion that consumers required shepherding.[34]

Reluctant to see consumers as passive victims, consumer organisations were apt to regard them as complicit in their own predicament. Their fallibilities and not only advertising 'as a market practice peculiarly susceptible to... the least admirable of human traits' were blamed. Thus as Nader's 1965 polemic *Unsafe at Any Speed* convulsed the auto industry, correspondents to *Consumer Reports* stressed driver as well as corporate responsibility for auto deaths.[35] An 'obstacle to the growth of the consumer movement has been the nature of the consumer himself', Warne said in 1961. What was needed was 'a degree of intelligence and skepticism on the part of the buyer – characteristics which [are] all too often absent.'[36]

This echoed progressive/socialist critiques and foresaw future anti-globalisation concerns. Warne sensed that 'advertising exercises a powerful educational impact upon... brand choices' and was, 'singularly effective (its appropriations exceed all monies spent annually for higher education).' Nader warned the National Press Club in 1966 that his foe 'GM last year grossed more than... any foreign government except the USSR and Great Britain.'[37]

---

[34] Roberts, *Wall Street Journal*, 12th July 1968 and *IOCU*, p. 2; Northcott, *Value for Money?*, p. 6; Nader, *New York Times Magazine* 18th January 1976; R. Millar, *The Affluent Sheep* (London: Longman, 1963), pp. 194-196. R. Wight, *The Day the Pigs Refused to be Driven to Market: Advertising and consumer revolution* (London: Hart-Davis, MacGibbon, 1972).
[35] 'Judgement at Mount Vernon'. in *Consumer Reports* (May 1966), p. 258. R. Nader, *Unsafe at Any Speed: The designed-in dangers of the American automobile* (New York: Grossman, 1965).
[36] C.Warne, 'The Independent Consumer Testing Agency: An international answer to brand name advertising', Zurich, 27th July 1961. Brooks 1/47.
[37] Warne, 'Economic impact' p. 6. 'Taming the Corporate Tiger', p. 134.

Knitting or bowling together?
Political contexts, social capital

CU was the product of a 1935 labour dispute when Consumer's Research attempted to prevent its staff from unionising. From this ensued accusations of communist influence, mostly from ex-Consumer's Research directors like J.B. Matthews, who became an aide to Joseph McCarthy and by the 1950s was 'an apostle of modern Conservatism'. CU's efforts in the 1930s to inform working-class consumption included a Labor Advisory Committee, involving Communists and labour leaders like John Brophy, the CIO secretary. *Consumer Reports* assessed labour conditions and relations in its product appraisals.[38]

The whiff of communism lingered around CU and was only formally cleared by the House Committee on Un-American Activities in February 1954. Until then it was red-baited. Leading figures like Warne, a 1930s radical, arrested as an ACLU activist and associated with a host of progressive international causes (and Henry Wallace's 1948 presidential bid), were dogged by association with communism. This was as true for Warne at Amherst College, the Massachusetts College where he was an economics professor, as in CU. Such progressive, respectable east coast academics (like H.H. Wilson) predominated on CU's advisory committee. If anything, CU's members seemed more radical. One said: 'All the subscribers I know are the same type – they all vote Democratic/Liberal.' They watched for any abuse of CU's ban on advertisers using its reports and insisted CU use its own testing facilities.[39]

If the *Harvard Business Review* could see 'vestiges... of the sensationalism of their early years', after CU was cleared of communism, it constantly affirmed that 'the central faith of the consumer movement is... that free choice lies at the very core of our economic system' (an instance, in its use of 'lies', of the double-edged epigram Warne relished). CU was righting the ways free choice was presently (due to corporate

---

[38] See, L. Glickman, 'The strike in the Temple of Consumption: Consumer activism and twentieth-century American political culture', in *Journal of American History* 88:1 (2001). C. Warne 'Report on Activities and Associations, 1930-53', Brooks 2/1, 2/2. The Labor Committee never met.
[39] 'Consumers Union: A Red front', in *The Freeman*, 28th July 1952; '*Consumer Reports* knows what's best'.

forces) askew, put great store by its internal democracy and was 'devoted to raising American living standards'.[40]

CU's sensationalist thunder was stolen by Nader, as it dealt more willingly in middle-class affluence. Not that it was immune to 1960s radicalism or what Cohen terms 'the third wave of the consumer movement' (after progressivism and the New Deal). This was sparked by Kennedy's 1962 Consumer message (promising consumers' rights to choose, be safe, heard and informed), the Thalidomide scandal and Nader's pursuit of (and by) GM from 1965. Nader's election to CU's board in 1967 (with other 'political' figures like Bess Myerson Grant) rejuvenated CU, doubling its readership between 1967 and 1971 and spurring it to launch a legal action in 1967 forcing the US Veterans' Association to release test data on hearing aids.[41]

'Nader's network' of organisations, chiefly the Centers for Auto Safety and Responsive Law (home of 'Nader's Raiders'), numbered 19 by 1971. 'We're still in the Jungle', Nader wrote in 1967, invoking progressive-era muckrakers to urge (and win) the updating of the (Sinclair-inspired) 1906 Pure Food and Drugs Act. Like CU, Nader stressed corporate reform besides consumer protection, believing that 'The American consumer is in a better position than consumers in other countries... No other country has anti-trust laws... an FTC or FDA or legislators that can be responsive to public needs when the public really puts on the heat.'[42]

Nader crashed onto the scene in 1965, but *Consumer Reports* claimed to have raised concerns about car safety just as early, and a 1965 piece revealed the radical edge beneath its moderate façade: 'Two hundred and fifty of the people who read this article... will be killed in a car crash within... two months... [It] is no longer possible... to report on autos without steady reference to their death-dealing and maiming character-

---

[40] Beem, Ewing, 'Business appraises consumer testing '; Warne, 'Report on Activities', pp. 26-37.
[41] Cohen, *Consumers' Republic*, p.345; 'CU puts on muscle'; 'Sending marketplace scamps'.
[42] 'Nader's network', in *Consumer's Newsweek* 1 (1971). 'We're still in the Jungle', in *The New Republic*, 15th July 1967, *Ralph Nader Reader*, p. 257. 'What makes Ralph Nader run?', *Readers Digest*, June 1973, p. 118.

istics.'⁴³ Whilst admiring Nader's 'sublime public relations work', Warne reckoned that 'if he left the field today, consumerism would carry on.' And on losing Nader's limelight in 1974, members urged CU: 'Stick to your knitting.'⁴⁴ Nader and CU's differences lay between CU's quiet, business-like approach and Nader's confrontational militancy. Warne found Nader's campaigns too *ad hoc* and scoffed at his notion of 'new citizenship', arguing, 'Civic duty is a feeling that has meaning for middle class housewives who want a little respite from the kids, but as an incentive for a broad-based powerful movement it just doesn't suffice.' Warne's vision was 'that consumer action groups could replace bowling teams and bridge clubs as a function of community recreation.' Far from culturally conformist or passive, consumer activity was then envisaged as socially cohesive, not destructive of bonds of trust. In the terms of commentators like Putnam, it was bowling *together* not *alone*!⁴⁵

The CA was mostly staffed by middle-class Oxbridge-educated, modernising social democrats, perturbed by the left's disinterest in addressing post-war affluence in anything much more than disdainful terms. This leftish make-up (Young for instance had been Labour Party Research Director and penned the 1945 manifesto) kept it off the Molony Committee appointed in 1959 to assess consumer legislation. Though some prominent 'one nation' Tories like Peter Goldman (CA Director 1964-87) also figured. And the CA was suspected of straying from the left since figures like Young were involved with the Social Democratic Party that split from Labour in 1981. Hilton argues CA's milieu was best characterised less in class, gender or political terms, than as a habitus of professional, suburban experts, moulding (less than moulded by) new consumption trends.⁴⁶

---

⁴³ 'Auto Safety', in *Consumer Reports* (August 1961); 'Car design and accident proneness', (April 1963); (April 1965), p. 6. Nader, 'The safe car you can't buy', in *The Nation*, 11th April 1959.
⁴⁴ 'Sending Marketplace Scamps', in R. Morse (ed.), *The Consumer Movement* (Manhattan, KS: Family Economics Trust Press, 1993), p. 246.
⁴⁵ D. Case, 'The Consumer Movement in the 1960s', Amherst College, BA, 1972, p. 108, Brooks 2/24 R.D. Putnam, *Bowling Alone: The collapse and revival of American community* (New York: Simon and Schuster, 2000).
⁴⁶ Black, '*Which?*craft'. M. Hilton, 'The Polyester-Flannelled Philanthropists: The Birmingham Consumers Group and Affluent Britain', in L. Black, H. Pemberton (eds), *An Affluent Society?* (Aldershot: Ashgate, 2004)

But CA's members were less radical than its leaders (the reverse in ways of CU's situation). Members' favourite newspaper was the conservative *Daily Telegraph*. In 1962, Gallup found most *Which?* subscribers were 'intent on value for money', but 'no evidence that members joined for the purpose of achieving reform... in the sense of manufacturing better goods for all.'[47] The CA's council was criticised as a 'self-perpetuating oligarchy' by the Molony Report and was reluctant to be elected by its members. CA leaders were concerned that their place in the consumer information marketplace was insecure. They were aggressive towards competitors like the Consumer Advisory Council and had feared the CC might compete with it as a testing organisation. The division of labour between testers, lobbyists and consumer information or education bodies, despite the profusion of 200 plus organisations by the 1970s, was more clear-cut in the USA.[48]

But there was no British Nader. Equally, Daniel Bell noted, there was 'no American figure like Michael Young'. Young's interests were too disparate and inclusive. The spectre of a British Nader, in the guise of Des Wilson, director of the homeless charity Shelter and the CC's director-in-waiting, was alleged to have prompted the CC's abolition in 1970. Why was there no British Nader? CU's tax-exempt status prevented it directly lobbying Capitol Hill (as Nader did), a pressure group function the CA combined with testing. The CA also sustained an acerbic tone (more Nader than CU), for example towards goods like the 1985 Sinclair C5 electric car.[49] Consumption's long-standing centrality to American identity made it a more sensitive, potent, political language, whilst Labour movement culture in the UK en-

---

[47] J. Mitchell, 'Results of Questionnaire' (1964). Gallup, *Which? Final Report* (May-September 1962). CAA A14.

[48] Cohen, *Consumers' Republic*, p.364. Thus US co-ordinating efforts like the National Association of Consumers or Consumer Federation of America were flawed.

[49] M. Young, *Social Scientist as Innovator* (Cambridge, Mass: Abt Books, 1983), p. ix. H. B. and S.V. Thorelli, *Consumer Information Handbook: Europe and North America* (New York: Praeger, 1974), p. 167; CA, *29th Annual Report* (1985-6), p. 9. Tax differences dividing lobbying and research/education, accounted for consumer group profusion.

sured critics of capitalism were commoner.[50] US political culture's comparative populism meant poking fun at authority was less novel than in the status-reverent British political climate. The CA's ironic, sceptical practice made politics more like consumerism (populist, Americanised) in its style as well as about consumer issues. As established authority (moral, political, commercial, state) was questioned during the 1960s, politics found growing competition for the electorate's attention.[51]

Transatlantic comparisons were eagerly debated. In an interview entitled 'The American Consumer – slave or rebel?' broadcast on the BBC's Third Programme in 1958, Reuel Denney discussed his work with British opinion pollster Mark Abrams. Denney worked with David Riesman on *The Lonely Crowd*, which forwarded an interpretation of growing US social conformity. Denney's recent book, *The Astonished Muse*, argued that the impact of mass consumption was more uneven or 'crumpled'. Conformity (which occupied Britons, Abrams explained, since they believed themselves to be following US trends) was a product of the power of business, the impact of immigration and desire to belong, and US egalitarian values. Conformity was being 'crumpled' by boredom (e.g. demand for innovative car designs), by careful spending by new suburbanites planning for children's education, by generational-regional differences (the young reading 'minority books', buying 'minority records') and resistance to the idea that 'spending' your time was the US way. 'Except for their consumption of beer, wine', college-educated New York journalists and San Francisco poets had, Denney felt, 'a kind of almost semi-monastic attitude towards hoop-la and glamour in the American merchandising scene.' Educating and informing consumers, either as shoppers or in how to use their leisure (the limited knowledge amongst the booming 'straw hat' theatre audiences was highlighted) was

---

[50] Though it was picked up by the AFL-CIO, see 'Spotlight on Consumer Protection', *Labor's Economic Review* vol. 5 nos 3-4 (March-April 1960), pp. 21-28.
[51] For a related argument, S. Wagg, 'Comedians and Politics in the United States and Great Britain' in S. Wagg (ed.), *Because I Tell a Joke or Two: Comedy, politics and social difference* (London: Routledge, 1998), pp. 244, 264-271.

agreed to be key. Western Europe was following US trends. Women and the young influenced consumption patterns, but less revolt was apparent since unequal social structures were the norm. Conformity's critics were thus often found amongst social elites. Abrams rejected them, arguing that 'conformity – uniformity in consumption – is a pretty low price to pay for escaping from poverty.' Upbringing was identified as another difference. Abrams contrasted the US focus on generational peer groups with Britain's more horizontal, parent-based traditions, and saw this as an inculcator of the notion that one should 'keep up with Joneses'. Britain, under Spock's influence, was again following in US footsteps. Both agreed consumption's promotion of 'self' freedom was of ideological relevance. Abrams felt that 'the itch for self government will seep over from consumption' and Denney stressed how the consumer 'becomes self-governing, not merely in the market place, but in the ideas that he relates himself to.'[52]

Conclusion

Warne wondered in 1965 'how economic historians or anthropologists will be able to explain in the year 2965 just what has happened to us...[or] account for our having the largest per capita debt for consumption purposes in our history after experiencing 20 years of what we have called unprecedented prosperity?'[53] The question has increasingly occupied commentators, aware that mass consumption did not translate into happiness and that affluence entailed social problems for the environment. This was highlighted during the 1960s in titles like Carson's Silent Spring and Reich's The Greening of America or in dietary and nutritional problems as wants replaced needs, and health problems like smoking or clinical depression. The shift from

---

[52] Transcript (21st July 1958, broadcast 14th August), Mark Abrams papers, Churchill College, Cambridge, Box 35, File 'Broadcasts, 1948-62'. R. Denney, *The Astonished Muse* (Chicago: University of Chicago Press, 1957). D. Riesman with N. Glazer, R. Denney, *The Lonely Crowd: A Study of the Changing American Character* (New Haven: Yale University Press, 1969 [1st edition 1950]), pp. lx-lxi details Denney's contribution.
[53] C. Warne, 'Consumer Credit', pp. 1-2, AFL-CIO Community Services Conference, May 1965, Brooks 1/47.

necessity to luxury raised expectations and the stakes of disappointment: this was the depression of affluence or High Price of Materialism.[54]

This was truest of the USA, where as Potter's *The People of Plenty* worried (as early as 1954), consumption and expectations that its frontiers would expand was embedded in the US identity. The consumers' republic produced some of the most sustained critiques and richest debates, pre-empting in topic (if not outcome) those elsewhere. CU was a vital resource amongst a growing body of criticism with transatlantic impact: Galbraith, Riesman, CU's charge that advertising damaged the countryside. Caplovitz's, *The Poor Pay More* (1963), a CU subsidised study of consumer credit in Harlem, aided the UK's 'rediscovery of poverty' by social policy researchers in 1965. Vance Packard's squibs, *The Hidden Persuaders* and *The Waste Makers* (akin to Chase's, *The Tragedy of Waste*, 1925), were popular in the UK. Packard's success, like CU's use of free choice to critique big business, was to deploy the sound bite style of his advertising quarry.[55]

Packard considered CU 'the... most potent countervailing force in the land.' But it is apparent that there were limits to consumer politics. Turner Morris' conclusions that, 'The well-to-do subscribe to CU, the poor do not', that legisla-

---

[54] R. E. Lane, 'Friendship or Commodities? Friendship, Consumerism and Happiness', in N. Goodwin, F. Ackerman and D. Kirou (eds) *The Consumer Society* (Washington: Island Press, 1997); J. Yudkin, 'Nutrition in the affluent society', in *Towards Scientific Management in the Home* (London: Council of Scientific Management in the Home, 1967) in Richard L.D. Morse papers, KSU, 201/8. M.B. Neuberger, *Smoke Screen: Tobacco and the public welfare* (Englewood Cliffs: Prentice-Hall, 1963). T. Kasser, *The High Price of Materialism* (Cambridge, Mass: MIT Press, 2003). R. Carson *Silent Spring* (Greenwich, Conn.: Fawcett, 1962) and C. Reich, *The Greening of America* (New York: Bantam, 1970)

[55] E. Angevine (ed.), *Consumer Activists: They made a difference* (New York: Consumers Union Foundation, 1982), p. 104. D. Potter *People of Plenty: Economic Abundance and the American Character* (Chicago: University of Chicago Press, 1954). D. Caplovitz, *The Poor Pay More: Consumer practices of low-income families* (New York: Free Press, 1963). V. George, I. Howards, *Poverty amidst Affluence: Britain and the United States* (Brookfield, VT., Elgar, 1991). Vance Packard, *The Hidden Persuaders* (London: Longman, 1957) and *The Waste-Makers*, (London: Longman, 1960), akin to S. Chase, *The Tragedy of Waste*, (New York: Macmillan, 1925).

tive efforts benefited the poor more than CU itself and that, 'the social reformers who started... Consumers Union hoped for a mass movement [but] they got a class movement', recommend themselves to the CA too.[56]

---

56 CU, This is CU; Morris, CU, pp. 52-3.

IV

The surprise of collective action: Consumer mobilisation in France, 1970-1985

Gunnar Trumbull

Introduction

In the 1970s, France saw the rise of an active and popular consumer movement. As early as 1972, a survey conducted by the National Consumption Institute (INC) found that 20 percent of French people over 15 said they were 'ready to belong' to a consumer organisation.[1] By the late 1970s, French consumer groups had become numerous, dynamic, and increasingly well funded. Another survey in 1978 found that interest in joining a consumer group had increased to 27 percent, and that two million French citizens had already become members.[2] Many of these were simply passive members, subscribing to consumer magazines or sending in annual contributions. But a growing number were grassroots activists. The Union Fédérale des Consommateurs (UFC), for example, a consumer protection group founded in 1951 that published the product review magazine *Que Choisir?*, began to take on affiliated local consumers' unions in the early 1970s.. These local unions, which took to the streets to carry out price surveys, product boycotts and protests, grew in number from 28 in 1974 to 170 in 1980,

---

[1] Dominique Pons, *Consomme et tais-toi* (Paris: Epi, 1972), p. 97.
[2] G.H. Gallup, *The International Gallup Polls: Public Opinion 1978* (Wilmington, Delaware: Scholarly Resources Inc., 1979), p. 365; *Le Nouveau Journal*, 28 September 1979.

with the number of local member activists growing over this period from 5,000 to 50,000.³ By 1982, a survey conducted by the journal *Nouvel Observateur* found that 76 percent of French people trusted consumer groups.⁴

The French consumer movement was not only popular, but also diverse. Many groups undertaking consumer protection in the 1970s had their origins as family associations founded in the 1940s, with a focus on defending family life and values.⁵ Others, including the Fédération Nationale des Cooperatives de Consommateurs (FNCC) and their product testing lab, LaboCoop, had emerged at the turn of the century from France's consumer co-operative movement. Originally set up as distribution channels for co-operative members, in the 1970s they began reorienting themselves towards the general consuming public. A third source of consumer mobilisation came from the labour union movement. The Organisation Générale des Consommateurs (ORGECO) was the first of these, created in 1959 to represent all consumers with a union affiliation. By the mid-1970s, France's individual labour unions began breaking away from ORGECO to create their own groups. In 1974 Force Ouvrière broke from ORGECO to form AFOC; in 1979 the communist trade union CGT followed suit, creating the affiliated consumer group INDECOSA-CGT. In 1981 the CFDT trade union created ASSECO-CFDT. Each of these groups used organising skills developed in the context of labour mobilisation to attract and motivate their own activist consumer memberships.

This high degree of consumer activism in France is surprising in three ways. The first reason for surprise is based on theoretical considerations. As a group, consumers should encounter many obstacles to collective organisation. Individual consumers have little incentive to contribute time or resources

---

³ Gunnar Trumbull, 'Strategies of consumer-group mobilization,' in Martin Daunton and Matthew Hilton, (eds), *The Politics of Consumption* (Oxford: Berg, 2001), p. 269.
⁴ This compared to only 32 percent who trusted trade unions. *Liberation*, 7 April, 1983, p. 14.
⁵ These groups included: La Confédération syncidale des familles (CSF – 1946); la Confédération nationale de la famille rurale (CNFR – 1944); l'Union des associations familiales (UNAF – 1945); la Fédération des familles de france (FFF – 1948); and la Confédération nationale des associations populaires familiales (CNAPF).

to a cause that may provide them only limited benefits. Moreover, the diffuse benefits of consumer mobilisation are often set against very specific costs for business.[6] To succeed, consumers have not only to organise, but also to do so more effectively than the businesses they confront. Moreover, consumers are themselves commonly also participants in production, either as workers, managers, or shareholders. To the extent that new consumer protections impose a cost on producers, even those individuals who stand to benefit as consumers may choose to forego such benefits out of concern for the losses that new protections might impose on them via their impact on producers.

The second basis for surprise is the dynamism of the consumer movement, particularly in France. France has traditionally been seen to be sceptical of the political and economic influence of intermediate associations.[7] Political scientist Peter Hall writes of French policy making: 'Aggregations of individuals and formal organisations outside the state cannot pretend to speak for the general interest. Their political status is suspect.'[8] This aversion to independent societal groups, compounded by the inherent challenges in organising consumers, would appear to make France a challenging context for dynamic consumer mobilisation. Compared to neighbouring Germany, for example, France was noted at the time for its distinct lack of mobilisation around issues such as nuclear power or the environment. How do we understand the associational dynamism of the French consumer movement, especially in a country characterised by formal relations linking citizens directly to the state?

The third surprise concerns the role of the French state in economic regulation. Between 1978 and 1983, France undertook

---

[6] Mancur Olson, *The Logic of Collective Action: Public Goods and the Theory of Groups* (Cambridge, Mass: Harvard University Press, 1965); Russell Hardin, *Collective Action* (Baltimore: Johns Hopkins University Press, 1982); Elinor Ostrom, 'A behavioral approach to the rational choice theory of collective action: Presidential address, American Political Science Association, 1997,' in *American Political Science Review* 92, no. 1 (1998).
[7] Michel Crozier, *The Bureaucratic Phenomenon* (Chicago : University of Chicago Press, 1964), pp. 316-317; Jonah D. Levy, *Tocqueville's Revenge: state, society, and economy in contemporary France* (Cambridge, Mass.: Harvard University Press, 1999), p. 13.
[8] Peter A. Hall, *Governing the Economy: The Politics of State Intervention in Britain and France* (New York: Oxford University Press, 1986), p. 165.

an elaborate experiment in consumer protection. Its goal was to allow organised consumer associations to represent the interests of consumers through agreements negotiated directly with producers and their trade associations. The state, in this approach, would step back from the negotiating table. On issues ranging from product labelling and safety to features of product design, this so-called *'concertation'* approach brought together consumer associations with producers and their trade associations to agree to mutually acceptable solutions to a variety of consumer concerns. Policies dealing with issues as diverse as truth in advertising, product labelling, consumer contracts, product design and retailing all became the focus of consumer-producer negotiations. By cutting out the government, this strategy of negotiated responses to consumer grievances was intended to lower the cost of regulatory oversight, while empowering consumer groups to represent their own interests in society. The idea was to grant consumers the same collective agreement provisions that workers already enjoyed. It would extend the principles of associational liberalism to consumers.

The strategy was not entirely novel. Both the Netherlands and Sweden had already experimented successfully with negotiated approaches to consumer protection. The Dutch consumer office Commissie Voor Consumentenaangelegenheden, created by the Ministry of Industry in 1964, brought together 9 consumer representatives, 11 industry representatives, and 2 union representatives to negotiate and set social and economic policy towards consumers.[9] Consumer claims were in turn handled by sectoral arbitration commissions representing both consumers and producers.[10] In Sweden, the office of the Consumer Ombudsman, a position created in 1971, represented the consumer interest in negotiations with industry.[11] The Ombudsman negotiated consumer contract terms with different industrial sectors,

---

[9] 'Les structures du consumérisme dans les états membres de la Communauté économique Européenne,' in *INC Hebdo* 729 (7 June 1991), pp. 3-16.
[10] Anne Fily and Philippe Guillermin, 'Les politiques de la consommation dans les États membres de la CEE', in *Revue de la concurrence et de la consommation* 70 (November-December 1992), pp. 46-48.
[11] Elisabeth Maillot Bouvier, 'L'Ombudsman dans la Politique de Concurrence et de consommation en Suède', in *Revue de la concurrence et de la consommation* 17 (1982), pp. 40-42.

worked with producers to resolve consumer complaints, and was empowered to bring legal suits on behalf of classes of consumers in special market courts.[12] Both countries offered a vision of consumer protection in which consumer and producer representatives negotiated mutually acceptable solutions that became the basis of national consumer protection policy.

But for France, a *dirigiste* state with deep commitments to regulating the economy, this experiment with a hands-off approach to consumer markets offers a third surprise. The 1970s in particular were a period of intensive government intervention in the French economy. Retailing and consumer product markets were being increasingly regulated: the 1973 *loi Royer* protected small traders against the growth of new '*hypermarchés*', and by 1976 the government was fixing prices for an estimated 137,000 products.[13] Despite this experiment with negotiated solutions to consumer grievances was endorsed on both sides of the political spectrum. Begun in 1978 under the third government of Raymond Barre, and strongly advocated by his economics minister, René Monory, the policy was also subsequently endorsed by the first administration of François Mitterrand, who saw it as an extension of the labour relations model to the realm of consumption. This chapter takes a closer look at this period, and the surprise of consumer mobilisation that characterised it.

The roots of consumer mobilisation

How were France's consumer associations able to overcome the collective action problems inherent in their economic role? One source of the proliferation of consumer associations was the increase in government funding that these groups received during the late 1970s and early 1980s. Combined government funding for consumer activities by family associations increased from 125,000 francs in 1974 to over 1.5 million by 1983 (in current francs).[14] Consumer groups that focused exclusively on

---

[12] Gérard Cas, *La défense du consommateur* (Paris: Presses Universitaires de France, 1975), p. 121.
[13] 'L'activité de la Direction Générale de la concurrence et de la consommation en 1980', in *Revue de la concurrence et de la consommation* 15 (1981), p. 4.
[14] This excludes funding for the government-sponsored group INC.

65

consumers, including the UFC, CSCV, and ANC, saw their funding increase over the same period from 80,000 to 1.3 million francs. Most impressively, funding to consumer groups affiliated with labour unions increased from 35,000 francs in 1974 to over 1.6 million in 1983. Even taking away the effects of inflation, total government support to independent consumer associations was seven times greater in 1983 than it had been in 1974 (see figure 1).[15] Beyond this direct support, the French government also provided indirect support in the form of services provided by the new para-governmental organisation called the National Consumption Institute (INC). Created in 1966, the INC published the results of comparative product tests, distributed information about product and consumer regulation to independent consumer groups, and helped to train consumer activists. Funding for the INC came directly from the government budget, with a growing share deriving from sales of the INC's own consumer magazine, *50 millions de consommateurs*.

Figure 1. Government support to consumer groups (millions of 1995 francs)

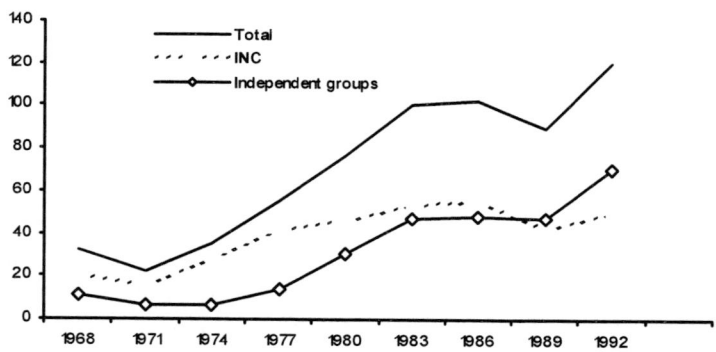

---

[15] Marie-Elisabeth Bordes and Sylvie George, *Politique de la consommation dans la Communauté Européene*, Memoire (Paris: Université de Droit, d'Économie et de Sciences Sociales de Paris, 1982), p 101. Noëlle Marotte, *Bilan et perspectives de la politique francaise a l'egard des consommateurs* (Paris: Conseil Economique et Social, 1984), p 20. Michel Bernard and Jacqueline Quentin, *L'avant-garde des consommateurs: Luttes et organisations en France et a l'étranger* (Paris: Editions ouvrieres, 1975), pp. 87-91.

France's consumer groups relied in part on government financial support, but they were also becoming more dynamic in response to the increasing delegation of quasi-governmental functions by the state. A government-sponsored *operation vacances* in the summer of 1976, for example, brought consumer groups together to sponsor 2,500 consultation points in 248 locations in the south of France in order to assist tourists with consumer grievances.[16] A consumer complaint service launched in November 1977, called 'Boîte Postale 5000' (BP 5000) for the address to which letters of complaint were to be sent, relied in part on consumer associations to help resolve disputes. While the programme was popular with the consumers who used it, it was not uniformly supported by consumer groups. Six national consumer associations, including all of the major family-oriented associations (CSCV, CSF, FFF, FNAFR), the labour union association ORGECO, and the dedicated consumer associations UFC and UFCS, boycotted the BP 5000 programme by refusing to handle BP 5000 cases referred to them.[17] Interestingly, their main complaint was that the central distribution system treated consumers individually, and so damaged their efforts to promote consumer mobilisation.

Apart from the government-sponsored services in which these groups participated, they also pursued their own activist agendas. The dozen or so national consumer organisations each published its own weekly or monthly journals. In 1974, the journals of consumer and family groups already enjoyed a joint circulation of nearly 2 million, of which 1.5 million was accounted for by *Le cooperateur de France* published by the FNCC, and 320,000 by *Que Choisir?* published by the UFC.[18] Most of these consumer groups also ran active public campaigns. Product labelling was a repeated theme for consumer groups, which frequently mobilised their par-

---

[16] *Un monde en mouvement: Les organisations de consommation* (Paris: Ministère de l'économie — comité national de la consommation, September 1980), p. 79.
[17] 'Six organisations de consommateurs contre les 'Boites postales 5000', in *Le Monde*, 26 Nov 1976.
[18] Michel Bernard and Jacqueline Quentin, *L'avant-garde des consommateurs: Luttes et organisations en France et à l'étranger* (Paris: Editions ouvrières, 1975), pp. 87-91.

ticipants to visit stores in order to evaluate the extent to which the regulations were being heeded. During the week beginning 20th November 1979, for example, 110 local affiliates of the UFC surveyed 27,735 shop windows and shelves in 160 cities in France. Mobilised under the slogan '*Pas vu pas pris*' ['Not seen not bought'], they found that 38 percent of the stores visited had not displayed prices on their products.[19] Such consumer group activities were in general well received, and the groups themselves appeared to enjoy the trust of the French population. A survey conducted by Sofrès in 1976 found that 4 percent of respondents trusted manufacturers to assure consumer safety, 20 percent trusted themselves, 37 percent trusted the state, and 34 percent trusted consumer organisations.[20]

Business interest in consumers

By the mid-1970s, France's major consumer associations were pushing for a more active role in promoting product safety. A 1977 survey found that 81 percent of consumer groups wished for a consultative role with industry.[21] But a dynamic consumer movement was not the only necessary ingredient for deploying a strategy of consumer protection based on negotiated standards. It also required that companies agreed to talk with these groups. And beginning in the early 1970s, French businesses and industry associations were increasingly willing to do so. Indeed, much of the initial contact between business and consumers took place at the initiative of the companies themselves. Their efforts to reach out to consumer groups were motivated in large part by a concern to better meet consumer demands. A survey of 550 French companies by the École Supérieure de Commerce of Lyons in 1976 found that a quarter reported having engaged in dialogue with consumer associations, although half reportedly still viewed consumer groups with hostility.[22]

---

[19] 'Une enquête de l'Union fédérale des consommateurs', in *Le Monde*, 12 December 1979.
[20] 'Les Français ne font pas confiance aux fabricants pour défandre les consommateurs,' in *La Croix*, 2 October 1976.
[21] 'Le Consumerisme', in *Libre Service Actualités* 632 (30 June 1977), pp. 135-136.
[22] 'Le Consumerisme, in *Libre Service Actualités* 632 (30 June 1977), p. 134.

Consumer efforts to reach out to companies were also frequently greeted with acceptance. One example was the case of Citroën. In 1978, two Citroën owners, a printer and a marketing specialist, joined forces to create the Comité de Défense des Citroënistes. They began by placing 10,000 notices on the windscreens of Citroën model CX cars in the parking area of a motor show in 1978, asking for owners' feedback and experiences with the car. Two thousand responded. Drawing on this initial pool of consumers, the Comité de Défense des Citroënistes began compiling the complaints and requests of users, which it then submitted to the company. Their goal was not to hurt the company, but rather to improve the quality of its products: 'We will not allow Citroën to produce goods below the standard of its reputation.' Citroën took these requests seriously, and worked to solve the particular problems they had raised. 'We accept this sort of confrontation,' said Citroën, 'it is part of our brand image.'[23]

When France established its first ministerial position focused on consumers in 1976, its new Secretary of State for Consumption, Christiane Scrivener, emphasised the value of incorporating consumer interests within the firm itself. She called on France's large companies to introduce what she called '*Monsieurs et Madames consommateurs.*' These would be company employees who, by representing the interests of product users, would play 'a role of constructive criticism' within the firm. This seemingly unusual government initiative represented an early commitment by the state to step back from regulation: 'The problems of consumption cannot be solved by a systematic intervention by the state,' said Scrivener.[24] It did not, however, prove particularly successful. Despite the pressures that were placed on firms to create such consumer advocacy departments, surveys showed that

---

[23] 'Les contestataires amoureux', in *Le Monde Dimanche*, 25 November 1979.
[24] 'Le Service consommateurs prend peu à peu figure dans l'entreprise,' *Les Echos*, 3 May 1979; Christiane Scrivener, 'Pour un 'service consommateurs' dans les entreprises', in *Les Notes Bleues du Service de l'information du Ministére de l'économie et des finances*, 6 April 1977; Jean-Marc Biais, 'L'Etat s dépense pour les consommateurs', in *La Vie Française* 30, January 1978, p. 6.

only 17 companies had such departments in 1976, 25 in 1978, and 30 in 1979.

At the same time that individual companies were increasingly interacting with groups of consumers, industry associations were also interested in making contact with France's officially registered consumer associations. One early experiment had shown that such negotiated approaches to consumer protection could work. Beginning in September 1970, France's largest employers' association, the CNPF, collaborated with the INC to create the Association Française pour l'Étiquetage d'Information (AFEI), a nonprofitmaking organisation in the public interest that designed and distributed model product labels.[25] In 1973, consumer associations also gained access to the board of directors of AFNOR, France's product standard setting body. Some early regional agreements also showed promising signs of success. In Alsace, for example, the consumer association Associations des Consommateurs Organisés (ACOR), with 130,000 families as members, signed agreements directly with retailers calling, among other things, for them not to charge more than 25 percent profit margins, and for them to open their accounts to a new Commission of Users. In exchange, ACOR provided them with its label to be included in their advertising, and advertised on their behalf in their own journal, *Le Consommateur*, which had a circulation of 80,000.[26]

These early success stories led France's central industry associations to open regular discussions with consumer associations. Over the period between 1971 and 1973, for example, the association of small and medium firms, CGPME, met with the INC, the UFC, and ORGECO to discuss consumer issues, but without coming to any agreements.[27] In 1973 the Paris Chamber of Commerce and Industry (CCIP) proposed

---

[25] AFEI was eliminated in 1984. Pierre Frybourg, (president of AFEI) 'L'Etiquetage d'Information,' in *Revue de la concurrence et de la consommation* 12 (1980), pp. 14-16. 'L'Etiquetage informatif vous aide dans vos achats,' in *Information Consommation Or-Ge-Co* 27 (March-April 1978), pp. 3-4. Jacques Dubois 'L'affichage des prix ... ne doit etre qu'un premier pas', in *Information Consommateur* 72/1, pp. 3-4.
[26] Dominique Pons, *Consomme et tais-toi* (Paris: Epi, 1972), p. 98.
[27] Marcel Garrigou, *L'Assaut des Consommateurs pour changer les rapports producteurs – vendeurs – consommateurs* (Paris: Aubier-Montaigne, 1981), pp. 53-54.

the creation of a new Centre de Concertation Industrie Commerce Consommateur (CCICC) that would bring together consumers and producers within the context of the CCIP. One of its goals would be to show 'that the protection of consumers is an essential goal of producers and distributors and that state intervention is not always indispensable for resolving problems of consumer information and protection.'[28] This initiative was also never achieved.

Real progress began in 1974, when, in the context of the first oil shock, CNPF president François Ceyrac announced that the CNPF wished to work together with consumers.[29] The following year the CNPF appointed Paul Simonet as head of a new Commission on Industry, Commerce and Consumption (CICC), with the goal of presenting a united front to consumer organisations. Simonet appears to have been extremely open to constructive discussions with consumer groups. 'Consumerism is a deep and durable movement that corresponds to the evolution of society,' he announced, 'and with which we must establish an open and constructive dialogue.'[30] The CNPF was, in the words of Simonet, 'very open to all forms of *concertation*, especially in the domain of information.'[31] It was a view shared by many members of the CNPF, as well. Jean-Georges Marais, for example, the director of customer relations at Air France, affirmed in 1977 that *concertation* with consumer groups was 'indispensable'.[32]

---

[28] 'que la protection des consommateurs est un objectif essentiel des producteurs et des distributeurs et que l'intervention de l'etat n'est pas toujours indispensable pour resoudre leurs problemes d'information et de defense.' Chambre de commerce et d'industrie de Paris, 'Problèmes de la consommation,' rapport présenté au nom de la Commission du Commerce Intérieur par H. Ehrsam Adopted 24 May 1973, p. 15.
[29] Marcel Garrigou, *L'Assaaut des Consommateurs pour changer les rapports producteurs – vendeurs – consommateurs* (Paris: Aubier-Montaigne, 1981), pp. 53-54.
[30] Gérard Lavergne, 'Eux, les clients,' in *CNPF Patronat* 429 (November 1981), p. 22.
[31] '...nous sommes tres ouverts a toute forme de concertation, plus particulierement dans le domaine de l'information...'; 'Opinions sur la fonction consommation et la libre entreprise,' in *Humanisme et Entreprise* 102 (April 1977), p. 16.
[32] 'Je voudrais affirmer qu'une concertation est indispensable.' Jean-Georges Marais, 'Le consommateur, cet inconnu?' in *Humanisme et Entreprise* 102 (April 1977), p. 69.

Government support for negotiations

By the mid-1970s, the French government began to take an interest in consumer-business negotiations. In 1974, National Consumer Committee (CNC) president Francis Pécresse requested the creation of a special working group on *commerce-consommation* to consider approaches to consumer protection. That group proposed to put in place in Toulouse a trial forum for consumer-producer negotiations. The new organisation, called Comité de Recours et d'Information Commerce Consommation (CRICC), was set up in 1975. Consumers were represented by two family-focused consumer groups, as many national consumer groups still refused to sit down at the table with businessmen. On 24th March 1976 the first meeting took place, with Chistiane Scrivener, France's new Secretary of State for Consumption, attending. It was the first truly equal meeting of consumers and producers in France, and resulted in agreements covering laundering and furniture retailing.[33] In another sign of growing government interest in consumer-producer negotiations, in 1975 the Commisariat du Plan created a new Consumption Committee that would address consumer issues for the first time in the Seventh French Plan. Consisting of consumer and producer representatives, the committee concluded that France should support the development of a dialogue between consumers and producers, although business representatives to the committee also reported a 'certain climate of hostility' among the consumer representatives to the Consumption Committee.[34]

The third Barre government, inaugurated in 1978, placed consumer groups firmly at the centre of its consumer protection policy. Instead of relying on government administration to meet consumer demands, the new economics minister René Monory called instead for consumer associations to function as a counter-force to industry: 'the consumer counter-force must

---

[33] Marcel Garrigou, *L'Assaaut des Consommateurs pour changer les rapports producteurs – vendeurs – consommateurs* (Paris: Aubier-Montaigne, 1981), pp. 161-162.
[34] Commisariat General du Plan, in *Rapport du comité Consommation: Préparation du 7e plan* (Paris: Documentation Française, 1976), p. 16. Jacques Dubois, 'Les consommateurs dans le 7ème plan', in *Information Consommation OR-GE-CO* 15 (March-April 1976), pp. 1-2.

be developed.'[35] The innovation of the Monory programme in these early efforts was to encourage collaboration on all aspects of the production process, something that the CNPF had long opposed. Monory charged the formerly neutral INC to support consumer associations to 'counterbalance the technical skill of producers and the effects of advertising.'[36] Consumer associations in this new confrontational approach were to be full partners in the production process, not only in providing product information, but also in defining product quality and price.[37] To this end Monory called for state funding to consumer associations to be quadrupled, from 1 million francs in 1978 to 4 million in 1989.[38] Monory, who liked to refer to himself as the 'minister of consumption,' gave actual authority over consumer issues to Danièle Achach, head of the newly created consumption mission within the economics ministry's Direction de la Concurrence et de la Consummation [Competition and Consumption Agency].[39]

By 1979, the CNPF had announced that it was ready to discuss broad consumer protection issues with consumer groups. Under the new initiative, the CNPF's CCIC held regular meetings with consumer associations from November 1979 to March 1981. They discussed standards for advertising, auto sales, after-sales service, furniture, and many more topics.[40] While decisions arrived at through these discussions were voluntary, companies that accepted negotiated standards could advertise their compliance as a selling point. Still concerned about the voluntary nature of these agreements, consumer groups were not content to limit their negotiations to the CNPF. They therefore also approached

---

[35] René Monory, *Inauguration des Locaux de L'institut national de la consommation* (Paris: Ministre de l'economie, Service de l'information, March 1979), p. 3.
[36] Gisèle Prevost, 'Consommation: 'l'agressivité' de l'INC préoccupe de plus en plus le CNPF,' in *Les Echos*, 28 May 1979.
[37] Jean Marchand, 'M. Monory veut des consommateurs puissants', in *La Croix*, 28 September 1979.
[38] 'René Monory: Davantage de moyens pour informer les consommateurs', in *Démocratie Moderne*, 22 November 1979.
[39] Formerly the *Direction de la concurrence et des prix*. Jean Marchand, 'Une 'mission consommation' au ministère de l'Economie', in *La Croix*, 17 June 1978.
[40] Gérard Lavergne, 'Eux les clients,' in *CNPF Patronat* 429 (November 1981), p. 22.

sectoral and regional industry associations to draw up separate negotiated agreements. By 1989, 49 voluntary accords had been signed between consumer associations and professional associations. Of these, 36 percent dealt with house construction, 20 percent used-car sales, 18 percent small retailing, 8 percent furniture and 6 percent dry cleaning.[41]

One such sectoral agreement dealt with standards of advertising. Between 1980 and 1983, the Conseil National de la Publicité (CNP) negotiated with consumer associations to set standards for the advertising industry. The meetings brought together 11 consumer organisations and 11 representatives of the media, plus the INC, BVP, and RFP. The professionals favoured the discussions, saying that it helped them, among other things, to keep track of the interests of consumer groups on issues that could change over time.[42] Another voluntary agreement was signed between consumer associations and UDAC, France's largest retail store association. According to this agreement, retailers following a set of negotiated guidelines would be allowed to put a sticker of a red, white and blue fleur-de-lis in their shop windows that read: *'Engagement du commerce, j'adhère'* ['I participate in the retail agreement'].[43] The negotiated guidelines included marking discounts as a percentage of the proper price, indicating prices *tout compris* (including services and other charges), clearly displaying information about after-sales service, and a guarantee to replace goods that did not function properly or were damaged in transit. Like many such accords, the programme was well received but not very widely used. An April 1981 study by the UDC of 663 stores in Marseilles found that only 27 stores (4 percent) had placed the *fleur tricolore* in their windows.[44]

Industry was happy with these early experiments with negotiated consumer protection as long as they primarily concerned issues of consumer information. But Monory intended to extend their scope to cover aspects of quality as well. One such effort focused on integrating consumer asso-

---

[41] 'Accords négociés entre associations de consommateurs et professionels,' *INC Hebdo* 624 (3 February 1989): 14.
[42] 'La guerre est finie,' in *CNPF Patronat* 447 (July 1983), pp. 71-72.
[43] 'La charte 92,' in *50 Millions de Consommateurs* 122 (February 1981).
[44] *Consommateurs Actualité* 282 (3 April 1981).

ciations into the process of setting product quality standards. The law on consumer information of 10 January 1978 provided for so-called *certificats de qualification* [quality certificates], a set of standard product labels intended both to guarantee a reasonable minimum standard of quality, and to provide an objective measure of certain dimensions of quality.[45] Research centres that issued these certificates would be approved by the Ministry of Research and Industry, and were required to include all of the social partners (producers, labour, consumers) in designing the certificates.[46] Under the quality certificates programme, consumers were invited to sit on the committees that would decide on appropriate criteria of quality and set minimum quality thresholds. Qualifying products would display a letter 'A' inside a hexagon, printed at the bottom of the quality certificate. The government's goal was to have all products labelled in this way by 1981. But the project became increasingly contentious, and studies revealed that hundreds of product brands were unlikely to meet even the minimum quality thresholds.[47] As it became clear that it might put both businesses and their employees out of work, the programme was quietly eliminated.

The search for binding agreements

By the time François Mitterrand was elected president in 1981, tensions over voluntary consumer-producer negotiations had come to a head. Producers were concerned that consumer groups increasingly wanted to participate in negotiations bearing on product design decisions. Initiatives like the 'quality certificates' programme, although formally a labelling programme, increasingly impinged on product quality and design features in a manner that industry felt was unduly intrusive. Consumers, for their part, were frustrated with businesses' unwillingness to adopt the voluntary standards negotiated by the industry associations to which

---

[45] Jean Calais-Auloy, *Droit de la Consommation* (Paris: Editions Dalloz-Sirey, 1992).
[46] Noëlle Marotte, *Bilan et perspectives de la politique francaise a l'egard des consommateurs* (Paris: Conseil Economique et Social, 1984), pp. 93-99.
[47] Elisabeth Rochard, 'Pour informer les consommateurs: Un 'certificat de qualification',' in *Le Matin*, 27 Jun 1979.

they belonged. In January 1980, 11 national consumer associations wrote a public letter renouncing participation in collective agreements until a formal enforcement mechanism was established.[48] Their answer came with the victory of the Socialist Party, which in 1981 put a new emphasis on collective agreements as a means of consumer protection. Mitterrand signalled the importance of this initiative by creating a Ministry of Consumption, to which he appointed Catherine Lalumière as Minister.[49] In September of 1981, Lalumière affirmed her support for the negotiation approach to consumer protection: 'I believe that we can do nothing with individual consumers in the state of nature, nor if all effort is concentrated at the state level.'[50]

Her efforts focused on ways to make agreements negotiated between consumer and professional groups legally binding. One approach, advocated by many consumer groups, would treat the consumer-producer relationship as analogous to the worker-employer relationship, with the state enforcing binding collective agreements.[51] Lalumiere therefore proposed to model consumer-producer negotiations on the 1936 labour law, which granted labour unions the right to negotiate contract terms at the sectoral level. Jacques Ghestin, a lawyer and spokesman for consumer groups, argued that the government should delegate authority over all aspects of consumer products, including product quality and the terms of consumer contracts, to negotiations among professional associations. 'In reality,' he argued, 'I don't see why professional organisations that are able to speak legitimately for their members about work conditions could not do the same in relation to sales conditions.'[52] Because a corpora-

---

[48] Didier Ferrier, *La Protection des Consommateurs* (Paris: Dalloz, 1996), pp. 80-81.
[49] Created by decree 81-704 of 16 July 1981.
[50] 'Je crois qu'on ne peut rien faire avec des consommateurs atomisés dans la nature et qu'on ne peut rein faire si tout est concentré au niveau de l'Etat.' In Josée Doyère, 'Un entretien avec le ministre de la consommation,' in *Le Monde*, 17 September 1981.
[51] Gérard Lavergne, 'Eux, les clients,' in *CNPF Patronat* 429 (November 1981), p. 22.
[52] 'En réalité on ne voit pas pourquoi les organisations patronales qui peuvent engager valablement leurs adherents quant aux conditions de travail, ne pouraient pas le faire quant a leurs conditions de vente.' In

tist strategy of this kind would have ramifications for all areas of consumer regulation, even some that had already been regulated, Lalumière created a committee, headed by the lawyer and consumer advocate Jean Calais-Auloy, to rewrite the full body of consumer law in France. Tellingly, no industry representatives were included on the committee.[53]

While the initiative to make negotiated agreements at the associational level binding was being developed, the government was also pursuing a more direct means of making consumer-producer agreements binding. Rather than devolving state powers to sectoral actors, this second approach sought a legal contractual status for agreements negotiated between consumer groups and individual companies. In December 1982, Lalumière modified the quality certificates programme created under the previous government to enable so-called 'contracts for the improvement of quality'. Under this new legal provision, products or services conforming to the norms established in negotiations between management and officially recognised consumer groups would be indicated with the *Marque 'approuvé'*, and include the 'A'-inscribed hexagon.[54]

These agreements had a mixed reception among consumer groups. The socialist and communist consumer groups strongly favoured quality agreements, and some companies even negotiated them through consumer groups affiliated with their own labour unions. Because these agreements took the form of contracts that were legally binding, consumers could resort to the court system to hold companies to their agreed standards. But not all consumer groups were satisfied. The UFC remained critical of the *approuvé* programme because they felt that it produced few results for consumers, and supplanted the more effective quality certificates programme that had been attempted by the Ministry of

---

'Négociation collective: Le point de vue des juristes,' in *Que Savoir* 43-44 (June-July 1982), p. 53.
[53] Chambre de commerce et d'industrie de Paris, 'La Politique de la Consommation,' rapport présenté au nom de la Commission du Commerce Intérieur par Messieurs Lefebvre et Blat, adopted 14 January and 11 March 1982.
[54] Jean Calais-Auloy, *Droit de la Consommation* (Paris: Editions Dalloz-Sirey, 1992), pp. 49-50.

Industry.[55] The communist-affiliated consumer group INDECOSA-CGT further complained that the government was not applying sufficient pressure on France's large nationalised companies to sign quality agreements with consumer associations.[56] Nor was the system as successful as its designers had hoped.[57] By 1985, only 59 companies had signed quality contracts with consumer associations, most of them with a duration of only one or two years.[58] Of these, 33 companies signed contracts to improve the quality of services; 26 companies signed contracts that applied to a total of 305 different products. A survey in 1986, four years after the programme was begun, showed that only 16 percent of the population recognised the *approuvé* certification.[59] While many judged the individual agreements to have succeeded, it became increasingly clear that such company-level negotiations could not satisfy the broader need for consumer protection.

Meanwhile, the effort to make negotiated agreements legally binding was meeting strong opposition. Both the business community and the Ministry of Justice found problems with the corporatist solution to enforcing consumer agreements. The business community argued that the analogy with labour contracts was a false one. They felt, first, that consumers were not dependent on producers in the way that employees were on their employers, since consumers faced few obstacles to shopping around.[60] Second, as delegates to the Paris Chamber of Commerce and Industry argued, they feared that the variety of interests in the professional community, which encompassed production, wholesale, retail and services, would put industry associa-

---

[55] 'Contrats d'amélioration de la qualité,' in *Consommateurs Actualités* 501 (21 March 1986), p. 19.
[56] 'Contrats de qualité,' in *Consommateurs Actualités* 498 (28 February 1986), p. 17.
[57] Jean Calais-Auloy, *Droit de la Consommation* (Paris: Editions Dalloz-Sirey, 1992), pp. 49-50; Didier Ferrier, *La Protection des Consommateurs* (Paris: Dalloz, 1996), p. 83.
[58] 'Contrats d'amélioration de la qualité,' in *Consommateurs Actualités* 501 (21 March 1986), pp. 17-19.
[59] 'Qualité: les consommateurs veulent un label unique européen,' in *Consommateurs Actualités* 604 (9 September 1988), p. 20.
[60] Josée Doyère, 'Des 'conventions collectives' de la consommation rendront obligatoires les engagements des professionnels,' in *Le Monde*, 5 December 1981.

tions at a disadvantage when they sat down at the negotiating table with consumers.[61] Jean Levy, who succeeded Paul Simonet in 1982 as head of the CICC, felt that binding collective agreements could inadvertently hurt producers, and therefore also ultimately hurt consumers. His concerns now extended even to labelling. In response to a negotiated proposal that retailers post the price-per-kilo and price-per-litre for foods, for example, he argued that this could lower the quality of products in the market by focusing consumer attention on price. 'This would be lead to an invasion of products of mediocre or bad quality.'[62]

The Ministry of Justice supported industry in opposing a corporatist approach to consumer regulation. While they felt that agreements between consumer groups and professional associations should be encouraged, they emphasised that these must remain voluntary. Consumer groups, they argued, were not sufficiently similar to trade unions. Whereas workers had a 'unity of life, unity of training, class consciousness, and direct impact on their work environment,' consumers remained necessarily dispersed and disunited.[63] Perhaps more threatening, a corporatist devolution of control of the sort being designed by the Calais-Auloy committee risked undermining important administrative authorities. Bodies such as the recently created Commission on Abusive Clauses would find their authority lost to consumer and producer groups negotiating beyond the scope of the state. In place of devolution they advocated non-binding approaches to enforcement, arguing that consumer-friendly brands such as FNAC and Leclerc had done very well in the marketplace by promoting a consumer-friendly image. By 1982, the movement to promote corporatist solutions to economic regulation, formerly a key component of the Mitterrand initiative, was already being scaled back.

---

[61] Chambre de commerce et d'industrie de Paris, 'La Creation du Conseil National de la Consommation,' rapport présenté au nom de la Commission du Commerce Intérieur par M. Gaucher, adopted 19 May 1983, p. 10.
[62] Elisabeth Rochard, 'Le CNPF ne veut pas de conventions collectives de la consommation,' in Le Matin, 19 February 1982.
[63] Ministère de la Justice, 'Observations sur l'eventualité de conventions collectives entre les organisations de consommateurs et les professionnels,' (Paris, 14 March 1980), p. 2.

France's turn to statism

Even as the first 'contracts for the improvement of quality' were being signed, the Mitterrand government was already undertaking a consumer policy U-turn, abandoning the negotiation approach to consumer protection in favour of direct state intervention.[64] Growing consumer frustration with the limited impact of the *concertation* initiative on business practice finally led the French state to step in to fill the regulatory void. It dismissed the Calais-Auloy committee to rewrite the consumer law. In its place the government enacted a set of strict regulations, enforced by new regulatory agencies, focused on consumer safety. The 1983 law for consumer protection created the *Commission pour la Sécurité des Consommateurs* [Consumer Safety Commission], modelled on the US Food and Drug Administration, to enforce a standard of product safety.[65] Under the law, government ministries were granted extraordinary rights to survey the consumer market and set product standards. A new *Direction Générale de la Concurrence, de la Consommation et de la Répression des Fraudes* [General Board for Competition, Consumption and the Elimination of Fraud], created in 1985, enjoyed extensive powers to visit and investigate companies, to seize documents, and to require that potentially dangerous products be recalled. Through these new agencies, and others that would follow, the French government quickly earned a reputation as one of the strongest voices for consumer protection in Europe.

The new statist regulatory approach to consumer protection brought benefits, but also posed challenges. The apparatus of the state did not always work rapidly or efficiently. The government's slow response to the risk of HIV infection through the distribution of untested blood to French haemophiliacs highlighted the risk of bureaucratic delay and raised concerns that the consumer interest might be hijacked by national industrial goals. But it also emphasised the new

---

[64] The '*Approuvé*' contracts remain a feature of the French product quality system, but are in limited use (only 24 such agreements were in use 2003) and have been applied mainly in services, especially the life insurance sector.
[65] Françoise Vaysse, 'Les anges gardiens de la sécurité,' in *Le Monde*, 14 April 1992.

responsibility taken on by the French state, as several officials and a minister lost their jobs when tainted blood entered the public supply. By the time the BSE scare emerged in the mid-1990s, French administrators were quick to take the risk seriously, and pushed for a prolonged ban on the import of British beef. Subsequently, on topics such as hormone-treated beef and genetically-modified foods, France embraced the studiously cautious precautionary principle of consumer safety to justify blocking these products from their markets.

This history of consumer mobilisation in France offers two broader lessons. First, despite conventional expectations, French consumers did organise in the 1970s and in many cases highly effectively. To the extent that they succeeded, it was in part through support from the state, in part through organisational expertise borrowed from the labour movement, and in part by drawing on France's own culture of social mobilisation and economic protest. Indeed the ultimate failure of the consumer groups' attempts to implement a negotiated strategy of consumer protection had its roots in the organisational weakness of industry. While industry associations at the national and regional level were willing to negotiate agreements with consumer associations, they appear not to have had sufficient influence over their members to ensure that these agreements would be respected. France's current statist approach to consumer protection resulted less from the organisational barriers that challenged consumers, than from the apparently greater challenges that producers faced in making the negotiation strategy work.

Secondly, researchers of public policy have typically perceived national consumer protection policies as emerging outside of a legitimate political process. Blinded by the assumption that consumer interests are too diffuse to organise, they have typically understood consumer-protection policies either as politically neutral regulation, or as protectionism. Thus the high degree of state involvement in consumer protection in France has commonly been perceived as a form of protection for domestic producers against foreign imports. But French consumer protection has a complex history, one involving interest-group mobilisation, policy contestation, experimentation and eventual success. France's policies today should therefore more appropriately be understood as the outcome of an explicitly political policy process, one that lends them considerable political legitimacy. (One of the most contentious issues for international trade, the European Union's opposition to hormone-treated beef, had its roots in a sustained consumer boycott orchestrated by French consumer associations in 1979.) When, with the failure of negotiations in the early 1980s, French consumer associations ceded authority over consumer protection to government agencies, they thereby placed a heavy burden of public protection on the French state. Thus, France's current strong stance on consumer safety, while certainly reflecting the interests of some elements of the French industrial and agricultural lobbies, also reflects an explicit social contract with its roots in a political process that started in the 1970s.

V

Corporate efficiency, democratic legitimacy and consumer-political integrity: Norwegian consumer co-operatives, 1970-2002

Espen Ekberg and Jon Vatnaland

The fundamental objective of consumer co-operatives is to serve consumer interests by establishing economic activities that are owned and controlled by the consumers.[1] Through voluntary and open membership, the consumers control how the economic activity is governed, and any surplus is redistributed to the members in accordance with their patronage or purchase. In other words, consumer co-operatives serve consumer interests by establishing *identity* between the consumer, the user of a given economic service, and the owner of the economic service.

By serving consumer interest through the establishment of consumer-owned and consumer-controlled economic activity, consumer co-operatives are fundamentally 'trapped' in a diverse set of dilemmas. Firstly, as economic actors, the co-operatives have to comply with the demands for *corporate efficiency*. Co-operatives can only serve the interests of the consumer through the operation of efficient economic activ-

---

[1] As the co-operative principles highlight, a co-operative is established to meet the members' 'common economic, social and cultural needs and aspirations through a jointly-owned and democratically-controlled enterprise.' Ian MacPherson, *Co-operative principles for the 21st century* (Geneva: International Co-operative Alliance, 1996) p. 7.

ity, as the very survival of the organisation rests on its ability to operate as an efficient corporate actor. Secondly, as organisations designed with the purpose of being controlled by their members, co-operatives have to fulfil the demands for *democratic legitimacy*. Democratic governance is a fundamental principle within co-operatives and cannot be disregarded without sacrificing the very essence of this distinct organisational form. And, finally, as organisations established to serve consumer interests, consumer co-operatives have to sustain a strong sense of *consumer-political integrity*. Without being perceived as organisations actually serving the interests of the consumer, membership will decline and the very foundation on which the co-operatives rest will disappear.

This article takes a close look at the history of the Norwegian Union of Consumer Co-operatives and tracks the changing nature of the relationship between corporate efficiency, democratic legitimacy and consumer-political integrity as the organisation has slowly entered the era of neoliberal economics in Norway. Through this endeavour, the article seeks to describe and understand how the balance between the movement's business side, democratic side and ideological side has been constantly debated and reformulated. The analysis also seeks to shed light on the question of why Norwegian consumer co-operatives have prospered so remarkably the last 30 years, contrary to their development in most other European countries.

Norwegian consumer co-operatives

The history of Norwegian consumer co-operatives dates back to the mid eighteenth century. Throughout the 1850s a limited number of consumer co-operative societies were set up in the largest cities, pushed forward by middle-class philanthropists who sought to spread the ideas established in the British co-operative movement among Norwegian workers.[2] Most of these associations were rather short-lived, but they became important precursors of a second wave of farmer-

---

[2] Iselin Theien, 'Socialism, liberalism or political neutrality? The balancing act of the consumer co-operatives in inter-war Norway', in *Journal of Co-operative studies*, 35:3 (106), pp. 167-182.

initiated co-operatives that emerged between 1865 and 1875 with the main aim of serving the interests of the rural population in their fight to become fully integrated into the modern commercial culture of consumption. Throughout the 1890s the co-operative movement, under the strong influence of the liberal lawyer Ole Dehli, experienced a third wave of expansion. And in 1906, the local co-operative societies established the Norwegian Co-operative Union and Wholesale Society, Norges Kooperative Landsforening (NKL).[3]

Despite the fact that the NKL was established as a wholesale society to the local co-operative associations, it was not until after the Second World War that the organisation actually became the main provider of wholesale services to local co-operative societies. By then, the number these co-operatives had risen dramatically, reaching a peak of 1165 societies in 1956, with more than 300 000 individual members.[4] In the years to follow, the NKL took a more active role in reducing the numbers of co-operatives by encouraging the mergers of local societies into larger units. And a more integrated co-operative structure was gradually established, with the NKL as the central wholesaler (as well as the producer of selected products such as coffee, margarine, and flour) and with local societies being responsible for retail activities. In competition with a private grocery retail sector characterised by fragmented and localised structures, the Union of Consumer Co-operatives gradually became the dominant provider of groceries within the Norwegian market.[5]

Thus, while the co-operative movement throughout Europe slowly but surely experienced a decline in the decades after the Second World War, Norwegian co-operatives flourished. This relative success was not limited to Norway, however, as both the Danish and Swedish co-operatives also saw a positive growth. And today, co-operative societies in the Scandinavian countries are a dominating force within Scandinavian retailing, with a membership encompassing about twenty percent of the total population and, through

---

[3] Ibid.
[4] 'Våre tall 1907-1906.' Statistics compiled by Tore Kristoffersen, Coop NKL.
[5] By the beginning of the 1970s, the consumer co-operatives had a total market share within the Norwegian grocery market of 24.8 percent (Annual Report, NKL 1973, p. 26).

the jointly owned food retail and non-food commodities concern Coop Norden, accounting for about 22.8 percent of the grocery market.[6] How did this positive development come about in Norway?

The 1970s

Contrary to developments in many other European countries, Norway experienced a booming demand during the 1970s. Oil exploration, which began in the mid 1960s, was gradually making its influence felt, and in combination with expansionist economic policies, investments, consumption and the production of consumer goods rose dramatically.[7] As a result, Norway had the strongest economic growth in Europe from 1974 to 1980.[8] This booming demand directly affected the Norwegian consumer co-operatives. In 1970 the total turnover of the NKL reached 1 billion Norwegian kroner (NOK) for the first time in history. Only five years later, in 1975, this billion that had taken the organisation 64 years to reach had doubled, and within another four years it had tripled. Local co-operative societies also experienced a strong growth in sales, from three billion in 1970 to almost 8 billion in 1979.[9] It is clear, however, that a high rate of inflation accounts for much of this dramatic growth. Total volumes of sales in society as a whole were also rising dramatically, directly affecting the sales revenues of the co-operative shops. Still, with a real growth in sales of about 30 percent, the market shares of the co-operative shops were stable at 25 percent, and the rise in total turnover made room for substantial investment both at the local level and within the NKL.

In spite of this positive development within the commercial activities of the co-operatives, the 1970s could not be characterised as a decade where the corporate activities of

---

[6] Annual report, Coop Norden AB, p. 7
[7] Jan Fagerberg, Ådne Cappelen, Lars Mjøset and Rune Skarstein, 'The Decline of Social-Democratic State Capitalism in Norway', in *New Left Review* No. 181, pp. 60-94.
[8] B. Furre, *Norsk historie 1914-2000. Industrisamfunnet – frå vokstervisse til framtidstvil*, (Oslo: Det norske samlaget, 2003), p. 229.
[9] 'Våre tall 1907-1906.' Statistics compiled by Tore Kristoffersen, Coop NKL.

the organisation were dominating. In fact, it rather seems as though the positive development within the business operations, pushed forward by favourable macroeconomic conditions, gave way to a stronger commitment within the movement to its role as a democratic association of consumers. Looking closer at the debates, meetings, annual reports and strategy plans, it seems clear that the main agenda of the consumer co-operatives during the 1970s was to promote the movement as a democratic consumer association. Both at the NKL congress (the central legislative body of the co-operative union) as well as in the routine activities of the NKL and the local societies, considerable attention was given to formulating and taking an active stance on questions concerning consumer politics.

In 1971, the NKL congress decided to instigate a 'co-operative consumer programme'. The programme, presented for the first time at the congress in 1974, and revised at the congress in 1977, clarified the governing principles of the organisation, and strongly emphasised that the wants and needs of the consumer should be the main guiding principle for how consumer co-operatives organised their economic activity. [10] As the chairman of the NKL board, Peder Søiland, clearly stated it in his speech to the 1974-congress:

> It is the consumers' various needs for goods and services that form the basic foundation for how the consumer co-operative movement will organise its production and retail activities.[11]

Furthermore, 'level-headed and realistic' consumption was established as a main goal for the basic activities of the movement.[12] This aim was to be achieved through consumer education, matter-of-fact product information, a socially acceptable selection of products and responsible marketing.[13] In the presentation of the revised programme in 1977, the

---
[10] Congress was during this period held every third year, and hosted about 300 delegates from local co-operative societies as well as from the NKL. See Stenographic report, NKL's 32nd Congress 1971; Stenographic report, NKL's 33rd Congress 1974; Stenographic report, NKL's 34th congress 1977.
[11] Stenographic report, NKL's 33rd Congress 1974, p. 197.
[12] Ibid.
[13] Ibid.

primary aim of developing a democratically governed economic enterprise was further highlighted:

> The primary aims are ... not simply economic advantages. We also need to keep in mind and remind ourselves of the fundamental demand of developing a democratically governed economy, in line with co-operative principles.[14]

In addition, and as an overall objective of the co-operative movement, the chairman stated the need to 'continue to develop a democratically governed economy to support and strengthen a viable democracy in our country.'[15]

As the 1970s were progressing, the corporate activities of the movement were thus supplemented by a revitalised ideological commitment, aimed at strengthening the role of consumer co-operatives as a viable consumer movement. As earlier indicated, this shift in focus might well be partly explained by the favourable economic conditions in which the co-operatives were now operating. Equally important, the 1970s also saw the establishment of a green movement in Norway, receiving broad popular support.[16] And within the political sphere, a radicalisation within the governing Labour Party led to a series of new initiatives aimed at strengthening the role of the consumer, for instance by restraining the progressive centralisation of the retail services.[17] As the Norwegian historian Edgeir Benum has highlighted, the 1970s was generally a decade characterised by a 'radical breakthrough' in Norwegian society. And it was within this framework of radicalisation that the Norwegian union of consumer co-operatives developed its revitalised consumer-political stance.[18]

At this point it is worth noting that a similar revitalisation of the consumer-interest aspect of the co-operative

---

[14] Stenographic report, NKL's 34th Congress 1977, p. 179.
[15] Søiland, Peder, 'Samvirke i tiden', in *Dagsorden, Kongressdokumenter, Representantfortegnelse*. Documents presented at NKLs 34th Congress 1977, p. 56.
[16] Edgeir Benum, *Overflod og fremtidsfrykt 1970-*. Aschehougs Norgeshistorie, bind 12. (Oslo: Aschehoug, 1998), pp. 28ff.
[17] Francis Sejersted, 'Norge under Willoch', in F. Sejersted, *Norsk Idyll?* (Oslo: Pax, 2000).
[18] Benum, op. cit., p. 28

movement also occurred in Sweden. From defining itself as an economic association established to serve the interest of its members, the NKL's Swedish counterpart the KF (Kooperative Förbundet), reformulated its governing rules, explicitly defining itself as a professional body for the promotion of the consumer interest in general.[19] As the Swedish social scientist Sun-Jon Hwang has demonstrated, however, these reformulations did not lead to a revitalisation of the actual consumer-political work done by the organisation. On the contrary, the 1970s saw a situation where Swedish consumer co-operatives handed over important parts of their consumer-political responsibilities (such as consumer education and product testing activities) to the public consumer council, Konsumentverket.[20]

Within the Norwegian movement, on the other hand, the renewed emphasis given to the NKL's responsibilities as a consumer organisation also had clear implications for its practical work. First of all, and following the principles grounded in 'the co-operative consumer programme', the 1970s saw a strengthened commitment within the NKL to intensifying its educational work with regard to consumers. During the decade, the NKL further developed its organisational capabilities concerned with education and information and launched a series of initiatives aimed at educating consumers on issues such as nutrition, consumer rights and product quality control.[21] In addition, economically-motivated plans for rationalising the structure of the co-operative societies temporarily came to a halt. The rationalisation plans, formulated in the late 1950s, had initially led to a dramatic reduction in the number of local co-operative societies. But, during the 1970s, local co-operators grew increasingly sceptical about the centralisation and loss of local control brought about by the rationalisations. The creation of larger units was believed to destroy the sense of local belonging among the members, weaken member influence and member

---

[19] Sun-Joon Hwang, *Folkrörelse eller affärsforetag. Den svenske konsumentkooperationen 1945-1990*, (Stockholm: Stockholms Universitet, 1995)
[20] Ibid. pp. 123 ff.
[21] Gunnar C. Aakvaag, *Mellom sosialdemokratisk modernisering og nyliberal individualisering. En studie av Forbrukersamvirket og medlemmene fra 1970 til 2003*, (Oslo: Institute for Social Research, forthcoming, 2004).

involvement, and curb the ability of the co-operatives to serve their mission as a genuine consumers' movement. Thus, while the number of local societies was reduced by 30 percent between 1960 and 1970, there was only a 15 percent reduction between 1970 and 1980.[22]

Throughout the 1970s there also emerged a growing concern among co-operators regarding the increasing geographical concentration of the retail sector at large, in particular in relation to the problems of maintaining a viable structure of local shops in rural areas. On these grounds, a decision was made at the NKL congress to establish an economic scheme for central subsidies to small, rural shops. The main reason given for this move underlines the clear determination within the NKL administration to act as a viable consumer's movement:

> [The] continuous closing down of rural shops may cause serious problems, if not to say catastrophic problems for the local population. ... It is on these grounds that we are very happy for the decision made here at this congress to help these vulnerable consumers.[23]

Thus, a general conclusion is that while the economic activities of both the NKL and local co-operative societies saw a quite remarkable development during the 1970s, the movement mainly focused on being a democratically governed association of consumers. This is not to say that the organisation disregarded its corporate responsibilities. During the 1970s, both the NKL and local co-operative societies invested heavily in new warehouses, in developing large department stores accommodating new consumer trends, and in renewing the existing structure of the co-operative outlets. But, when looking at the general principles governing the organisation and the range of activities employed, the wants and needs of the consumer were generally put at the forefront. The business endeavours were in this respect all treated as means to this end.

---

[22] 'Våre tall 1907-1906.' Statistics compiled by Tore Kristoffersen, Coop NKL.
[23] Vice president of the NKL board, Jarle Benum. Stenographic report, NKL's 33rd Congress 1974, p. 85.

When the economic growth of the 1970s stagnated at the end of the decade, however, the economic results of both the NKL and the local co-operative societies were immediately weakened. The sales revenues and operating profits of the NKL stagnated. And within the co-operative societies, average profits were reduced from 2.2 percent of total turnover in 1976 to 0.9 percent in 1984. Within the same period, the number of local co-operatives running into deficits more than doubled, from 88 in 1976 to 193 in 1984.[24]

Parallel to this economic downturn, increasing attention was given within the movement to how its economic activities were carried out. It is thus symptomatic that the revision of the co-operative consumer programme at the 1980 congress brought back the old plan for rationalising the structure of co-operative societies, in order to create a more 'cost efficient organisational structure'.[25] The revised programme also underlined the need to concentrate its educational work on generating a better understanding and respect within local co-operative societies with regard to the regulations and rules governing the organisation, and to highlight the corporate and organisational challenges that the co-operatives were facing in the new decade.[26]

The 1980s

While the 1970s saw a situation where a quite remarkable economic prosperity within the co-operative movement was followed by a strong commitment to formulate an explicit consumer policy, the 1980s became a decade where the consumer-political aspects of the organisation were pushed into the background. This came about at different levels and as the result of important changes in the political, the economic, the demographic and the ideological environment in which the NKL operated. Politically, a situation of stable social democratic rule was replaced by increasing support for the Conservative Party

---

[24] The Coop NKL archives at Kirkegata 4, Oslo, hereafter referred to as K4, 7A.4: 'Driftsmessig/økonomisk utvikling i S-lagene. 10 års oversikt.' Document presented at the NKL administration meeting, case 1.87b
[25] NKL, Annual Report 1980, p. 4.
[26] NKL, Annual Report 1980; Stenographic report, NKL's 35th Congress 1980.

and a gradual dissolution of established social democratic policies.[27] This affected the co-operative movement negatively, as Labour, since the early 1950s, had acted as an active supporter of the co-operative movement.[28] Within the new political landscape of the 1980s, political support for the co-operative movement gradually dwindled.

The consumer co-operatives also had to face the fact that the economic environment in which they operated was undergoing substantial changes. Markets were deregulated and competition within the grocery sector grew stronger. From being the only, partly integrated, national chain of grocery stores, during the 1980s the co-operative movement was met with competitors characterised by strongly integrated structures and with the financial strength to increase their market shares at an accelerating pace through the acquisition of existing shops. Finally, demographic and ideological transformations also affected the co-operatives. The increasing depopulation of rural areas challenged the strongest areas of co-operative business. Moreover, one could also argue that as far as the decade saw the gradual establishment of a more individualist consumerist ethos, in addition to a weakened support within society for the collective values of popular movements, the foundations of consumer co-operation were challenged.[29]

In addition to these external transformations, internal changes within the NKL also played an important role. In the early 80s, both the chairman of the board, Peder Søiland, and the managing director, Knut Moe, resigned. The two had been leading figures within the NKL for more than 25 years, and had thus contributed to a strong, coherent and stable

---

[27] Fargerberg et.al.; Sejersted.
[28] See Iselin Theien, 'Two phases of consumer co-operation in Scandinavia: Pre-war pluralism and post-war unification under social democracy', in *Consumerism Against Capitalism?* (Belgia: AMSAB, forthcoming 2004).
[29] See Ellen Furlough and Carl Strikwerda, 'Economics, Consumer Culture and Gender: An introduction to the politics of consumer cooperation', in Ellen Furlough and Carl Strikwerda, *Consumers against Capitalism? Consumer Cooperation in Europe, North America and Japan, 1840-1990* (Lanham: Rowman and Littlefield, 1999); Karl Henrik Sivesind, Håkon Lorentzen, Per Selle and Dag Wollebæk, *The Voluntary Sector in Norway. Composition, Changes and Causes*, (Oslo: Institute for Social Research, 2002), p. 2.

leadership within the organisation. As the two leaders resigned, the NKL was faced with a period of unstable and incoherent management. When the new management was finally in place by the autumn of 1982, the stage was set for a considerable revision of NKL strategy. The new managing director, Knut Værdal, immediately initiated comprehensive changes within the NKL administration, and put in motion extensive work to establish a long-term strategic plan for the organisation's business activities.

The strategic plan was designed to improve the economic output of the NKL by formulating a more 'aggressive marketing strategy'.[30] At the 1983 congress, the consumer programme of the 1970s was put aside, and the stage was set for a sharper focus on corporate operations. The new chairman of the board, Magne Bølviken, clearly expressed this change when addressing the 1983 congress:

> It is on the shop floor that the battle will be fought. It is here that the future of the consumer co-operatives will be decided. If the shops are doing well, the NKL is doing well... If the shops are properly run, more members will be recruited... It is on the shop floor that our position as a democratically governed enterprise based on the cooperative principles can be justified... Therefore: let's put our shops centre stage![31]

With this clear statement in mind, it should come as no surprise that the final content of the new strategic plan marked a clear shift in the balance between the NKL as a consumers' movement and as an economic enterprise. While the consumer programmes of the 1970s had been preoccupied with clarifying the organisation's perspectives on consumer politics, the strategic plan developed between 1982 and 1985, and presented to the congress in 1986, mainly focused on corporate issues. Besides highlighting a few goals and future plans for membership recruitment, as well as implementing a reduced version of the original co-operative consumer programme, the plan was purely a strategic corporate one, ana-

---

[30] NKL, Annual Report 1982, p. 11; see also 'Strategiplan for 1985-1994 for S-lagene og NKL.'
[31] Stenographic report, NKL's 36th Congress 1983, p. 78.

lysing the co-operative market potential and the existing conditions of competition, giving historical descriptions and analyses of sales, net profits and market shares, and presenting future plans for business expansion.[32]

As the strategic plan was finally presented at the 1986 congress, the economic results of the co-operative enterprise had improved, fostering a new optimism within the organisation. In general, Norway experienced a new boom in consumer demand. The Conservative Party, which had moved into office in 1981, pursued a strategy for economic growth in line with neo-liberal economic policies. A strong emphasis was given to stimulating supply by reducing growth in public spending, by cutting taxes for higher income households and businesses and by deregulating markets.[33] The result was one of a veritable boom in bank lending and investment, both for private households and businesses, again causing a substantial rise in sales revenues within the co-operative enterprise. The investment boom was also characterised by a strong growth in mergers and acquisitions within the business community. And this trend also manifested itself within the co-operative enterprise.

In the period from August 1985 to July 1986, the NKL decided to take full control of the Norwegian construction materials company Aspelin-Stormbull AS, the consumer electronics firm Økonom Elektriske AS and the fast-food chain Snappy AS. The investments amounted to a total of 302 million NOK. The acquisition of Aspelin-Stormbull alone represented an investment of 270.5 million NOK and was by that time the largest business transaction ever to take place within the Norwegian commodity trade.[34] The acquisitions were guided by the 1985-1994 strategic plan, clearly stating an ambition of expansion and increased market shares within non-food segments.

---

[32] 'Strategiplan for 1985-1994 for S-lagene og NKL.'
[33] Fagerberg et. al.
[34] K4, 7A.4: 'Kjøp av Aspelin Stormbull Bygg A.S. Beslutningsnotat.' Document presented at the NKL administration meeting, 29.06.86, case 275/86; K4, 3A.2 Box 6: Ytrearne, Egil: 'Norske Hamburgerrestauranter A/S, Økonom Elektriske A/S og Norgesbygg A/S. Del B – Melding frå NKLs representantskap til NKLs kongress. Tilråding frå mindretalet i arbeidsutvalet.' Document presented at the NKL council of representatives, 26/27 March 1990.

In the NKL's annual report for 1986, the year was characterised as 'the most eventful year in the recent history of the NKL.'[35] As for the economic investments (and the economic losses that soon were to follow), the mid-1980s were certainly eventful. However, it seems safe to argue that at this point business activities were eclipsing the co-operative role of being a viable consumer organisation. In this situation, membership recruitment and consumer politics were largely neglected. For example, less attention was given to compiling membership statistics, leaving membership numbers out of several annual reports. The reports thus gave no warning to the NKL that the number of members was declining for the first time in the history of the Norwegian consumer co-operatives.

This may help to explain the fact that by the end of the 1980s both the NKL and the local societies experienced a substantial economic decline. Sales revenues began to stagnate and the co-operative enterprise as a whole experienced a dramatic fall in net profits. In 1987, the NKL ran a deficit and, for the first time in the history of the NKL, the organisation could not afford to pay its annual dividend to co-operative societies.[36] The total deficit of the local societies was also rising dramatically, reaching a peak of 164 million NOK in 1988.[37] In the same year, the average surplus of local co-operatives reached an historic low, at 0.3 percent of total turnover.[38]

In addition, neither of the large investments made by the NKL in the mid 1980s turned out successfully. The investment in Aspelin-Stormbull alone, for example (ending in bankruptcy only two years after the acquisition was made) caused losses amounting to about 350 million NOK.[39] The

---

[35] NKL, Annual Report 1986, p. 9.
[36] NKL, Annual Report 1987.
[37] K4, 3A.2 Box 5. Notat til NKLs styre fra administrerende direktør, 'S-lagene 1989': 1. Document presented at the NKL board meeting, 6.7.90, case 98/90; K4, 3A.1 Box 1: 'Tapssituasjonen i S-lagene. Tiltak for å redusere NKLs tap på krav', p. 7. Document presented at the NKL board meeting, 24.5.89, case 60/89.
[38] 'Våre tall 1907-1906.' Statistics compiled by Tore Kristoffersen, Coop NKL.
[39] K4, 3A.2 Box 6: Egil Ytrearne, 'Norske Hamburgerrestauranter A/S, Økonom Elektriske A/S cg Norgesbygg A/S. Del B – Melding frå NKLs representantskap til NKLs kongress. Tilråding frå mindretalet i arbeidsutvalet.' Document presented at the NKL council of representatives, 26/27 March 1990.

failed attempts at expanding the co-operative enterprise into new areas of business further added to the economic downturn, and as the 1980s were approaching an end, the position of the Norwegian Union of Consumer Co-operatives, both as a corporate actor and as a member-based consumer organisation, was under severe pressure.

The 1990s

In 1988, Knut Værdal retired and was replaced by Rolf Rønning as CEO of NKL. The decision to hire Rønning, an outsider trained as a business economist, turned out to be a decisive one. Rønning initiated extensive changes within the organisation and by 1991 the economic downturn experienced in the late 1980s had been reversed.

The results were striking. Economically, the organisation produced results never seen before in the history of Norwegian consumer co-operatives. In a retail market strongly affected by increasing concentration and strengthened competition, the co-operative societies managed to maintain their 25 percent share of the grocery market. And net profits within the NKL rose from being negative in 1987 to an all-time high of nearly half a billion in 1995. The local societies also experienced a strong growth, with the average surplus in terms of percentage of total turnover reaching 2.6 in 1995, a result not seen since 1960.[40] This dramatic strengthening of the economic efficiency of the consumer co-operatives was accompanied by an historically strong growth in membership numbers. As figure one shows, in the period from 1989 to 1999, membership nearly doubled. And while it had taken almost a whole century to recruit half a million members, the co-operative movement spent only ten years recruiting almost another 500,000.

---

[40] 'Våre tall 1907-1906.' Statistics compiled by Tore Kristoffersen, Coop NKL.

Figure 1. Membership of Norwegian consumer co-operatives, 1907-2000.

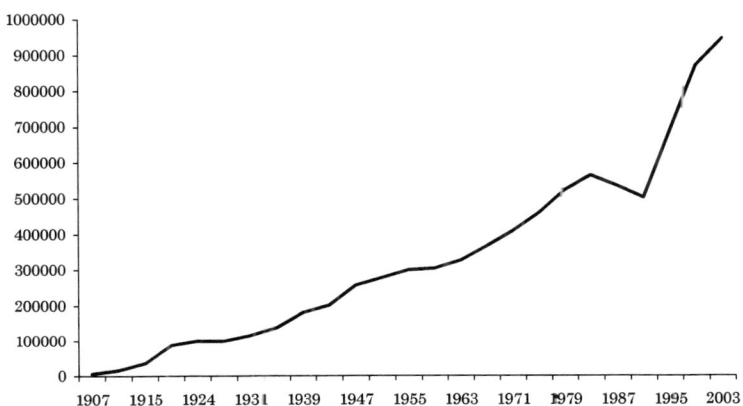

This parallel success of both the corporate and the organisational aspects of the co-operatives could be seen as an outcome of a closer attention given by the NKL to the economic benefit of recruiting new members. The idea was simple; membership created loyalty, and the more members recruited, the better the chances of commercial success. The membership aspect of the organisation was thus to a larger extent seen as a means to strengthening its economic results. Or, as the strategy plan presented at the congress in 1990 put it;

> [The] organisational aspects and the corporate aspects of consumer co-operatives are not to be treated as separate worlds, rather they give each other a unique distinctiveness and together they lay the grounds for competitive advantages.[41]

As such, the ideological, the democratic and the corporate aspects of the organisation were now to be treated as mutually reinforcing elements. And this linking of the demands for corporate efficiency with the aspects of consumer-political integrity and democratic legitimacy could be regarded as laying the foundations for the successful development in the 1990s.

An important conclusion is thus that the uniquely positive development of Norwegian consumer co-operatives dur-

---

[41] K4, 3A.2 Box 4: *Forbrukersamvirket i 90-årene*. Document presented at the NKL Congress, 1990, p. 4.

ing the 1990s may be explained by the ability of the movement to overcome the inherent dilemmas of the co-operative organisational form. At the same time, it seems clear that important aspects concerning the very nature of the co-operative movement were transformed but partly weakened by the same process. As a consequence of the corporate strategies employed, it could, for example, be argued that the democratic governance defining the essence of the co-operative enterprise was severely weakened. In addition, the notions of membership and consumer interests were adapted to serve the logic of market performance. This process occurred at different levels.

First of all, the NKL tried to bridge the gap between its responsibilities towards members and the need for efficiency in its economic activities by making membership a competitive advantage. This move was, however, dependent upon a significant reformulation of the notion of membership in itself, where a stronger emphasis on members as customers mainly seeking economic advantages from their membership became essential. Even though the NKL annual report from 1990 stated that 'the members and their interests as consumer are still at the centre stage for the organisations activities', it was at the same time highlighted that among the members, there had been a 'shift in values from the "old co-operator" who strongly identified himself with the co-operative ideology, to the busy people of today who have as their main interest making a profitable deal.'[42] On these grounds the notion of the consumer interest was reduced to the actual economic gains one could extract from being a member. The notion of membership thus went through a process of 'de-ideologisation', by which the member was to a greater extent treated as a customer rather than as a participant in a democratically governed organisation. A conclusion is thus that while the co-operative movement during the nineties was successful in recruiting members, and managed to exploit its members as a competitive force, the rhetoric of membership and consumer interest was significantly transformed.[43]

At the same time, several of the strategic choices that were made in this period, and that were pivotal in shaping the suc-

---

[42] NKL, Annual report 1990, p. 2.
[43] For a more extensive analysis, see Aakvaag.

cess of the co-operatives, led to a weakening of the organisation's democratic decision-making structure. A few examples should illustrate this point. Firstly, one important reason for the movement's economic success in the 1990s was the strategic decision to reorganise the business activities of the co-operative system. In the course of a few years the retailing business was reorganised into a chain-based system where local societies continued to have responsibility for shops, but where the NKL took a more active role in establishing and implementing a common strategy and a common branding of the outlets.[44] In close connection with this, the whole distribution system was reorganised to make sure that the different food chains were selling parallel products. By implementing such a centralised system, the NKL was able to realise large gains through economies of scale and by taking back control from the producers.[45] The success of this strategic move came at the expense of local influence. The local co-operative societies had to adhere to the centralised management of the chains, and lost the authority to shape the outlets as they wished.

Another important aspect of the strategies formulated by the NKL at the beginning of the 1990s was the idea of creating a co-operative conglomerate, based on the vision of offering the consumer the broadest possible range of goods and services. This strategy led to a series of attempts at establishing a wide range of non-food activities. During the 1990s, the NKL acquired or established joint ventures with a series of different companies, ranging from casual clothing chains, furniture chains, sports clothing, construction materials and jewellery.[46] The idea of the co-operative movement selling non-food products was not something completely new, as the local co-

---

[44] In the following years, four different food chains were established; 'Coop Marked', with a focus on proximity to the customer, and a product range that was supposed to cover everyday needs; 'Coop Mega', a supermarket chain offering a varied range of products from all over the world; 'Coop Prix', offering proximity and convenient shopping at fixed, low prices, and finally 'Coop Obs!', a so-called 'hypermarket' chain, selling a broad range of products from food to clothes, shoes, sports equipment and other non-food products (Coop Norden AB, Annual Report 2002).
[45] Espen Ekberg and Jon Vatnaland, *Visjonen som brast. Forbrukersamvirkets møbelsatsing 1993-2001*. (Oslo: Institute for Social Research, 2003), p. 5.
[46] Ekberg and Vatnaland.

operative societies already had a long tradition of offering non-food merchandise. What was new about the strategic expansion and conglomeration, first seen in the mid-1980s and then resumed in the early 1990s, was that the NKL took on a much more prominent role. Instead of expanding the existing activities of local societies, growing 'organically' into new areas, the NKL acquired existing, private firms and established them as daughter companies, joint stock companies or franchise outlets controlled by the central organisation itself. Unlike before, non-food merchandise was now to be sold from independent outlets separate from the local co-operative societies, the consequence being that local societies and their members totally lost control over the running of the shops.

Intensified centralisation and rationalisation of the structure of local co-operative societies further weakened the possibility of members having a real influence on the daily activities of their 'local' co-operative. In the period from 1990 to 2002, the number of co-operative societies fell by almost 50 percent. As the number of members increased dramatically in the same period, the average number of members of each local co-operative rose correspondingly. As such, the ability of each member to have a say in his or her local co-operative was equally reduced. The actual development is clearly illustrated in figure two below.

Figure 2. Average number of members of each co-operative society, 1960-1999.

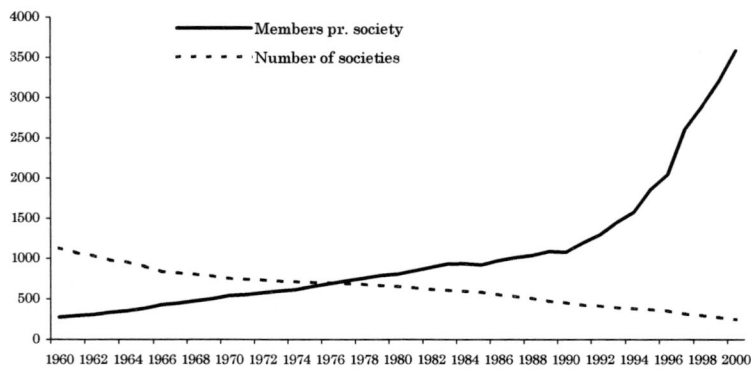

In conclusion, the 1990s saw a development where the NKL administration pushed forward a strategy resting on an attempt at combining demands for corporate efficiency with demands for consumer- political integrity, to create competitive advantage. The results were in many respects successful, both when it came to economic development and in terms of membership recruitment. The ability of each member to influence the decision-making process within the co-operative movement seems, however, to have been weakened in this process of growth. And the rhetoric of membership had to be fundamentally transformed, making it a competitive advantage for the business activities. In many respects, the development can be seen as one where the goals and the means of the organisation had changed status, where the economic activity had become the end and the idea of consumer interests the means.

Concluding remarks

Consumer co-operatives constitute a distinct way of organising consumer interests. While serving the interest of the consumer is their main objective, co-operatives also have to accommodate demands for corporate efficiency, as well as maintaining a truly democratic decision-making structure. The fundamental dilemma of reconciling these three demands has been at the centre stage of the Norwegian co-operative movement throughout the last 30 years.

Looking at the development within a broad framework, it seems clear that the question of how the organisation has dealt with this dilemma affords important insights into the question of how it has managed to maintain such a strong position. The detailed history of Norwegian consumer co-operatives has at least shown how the comparatively unique development of this movement has been based on a constant adjustment (and readjustment) of the balance between being an efficient corporate actor on the one hand, and a truly democratic association with integrity as a credible consumer movement on the other.

Recent developments in the Scandinavian co-operative movement have given a new direction to how this dilemma is handled. In 2002, the Norwegian, Danish and Swedish consumer co-operatives decided to merge their business activities to create a jointly owned Scandinavian food retail and non-food commodities concern, Coop Norden AB. By signing the agreement, considerable changes had to be made within the Norwegian co-operative organisation as a whole. Most fundamentally, large areas of corporate activity that had traditionally been the responsibility of the NKL, such as the entire wholesale operation, the management of warehouses and chains, the marketing apparatus and industrial operations, were transferred to Coop Norden AB. These activities were again redistributed to Coop Norge AS, which was established as a wholly owned subsidiary of Coop Norden AB.

In effect, the establishment of Coop Norden AB led to an organisational separation within Norwegian consumer co-operatives of the parallel roles of being a democratically governed consumer organisation on the one hand (this now being the main responsibility of the NKL), and a corporate actor providing goods and services to its members on the other (now taken care of by Coop Norge AS). Thus, at present, Norwegian co-operatives have implemented an organisational structure where the competing logics of democratic governance, consumer politics and market performance have been organisationally separated. The business activities have been fully detached from the ideological activities, and, as a consequence, the scope for members to have a genuine influence on how business operations are carried out has been further reduced. The question that still remains to be answered is what consequences this strategic shift will have for the future of the organisation. Will the movement manage to retain its integrity and legitimacy as a democratic consumer association, or will the organisational separation of the three basic pillars of consumer co-operatives gradually push the organisation towards more traditional models for doing business?

Contributors

Lawrence Black is Lecturer in Modern British History at the University of Durham. He is the author of 'The Political Culture of the Left in Affluent Britain, 1951-1964: Old Labour, New Britain?' (Palgrave, 2003) and co-editor of 'An Affluent Society? Britain's postwar Golden Age Revisited' (Ashgate, 2004)

Espen Ekberg took his M.Sc. degree in Sociology at the University of Oslo in 2002. He is currently a Ph.D student at the Department of History/University of Oslo. Ekberg has mainly been working within the field of economic sociology/contemporary economic history. His most recent publication is the book *Næringslivet mellom marked og politikk*, which he co-authored with Fredrik Engelstad, Trygve Gulbrandsen and Jon Vatnaland (Engelstad et.al. 2003). At present, Ekberg is participating in a broad project studying the history of the Norwegian consumer co-operatives in Norway.

Matthew Hilton is Senior Lecturer in History at the University of Birmingham. He is the author of Smoking in British Popular Culture, 1800-2000 (Manchester University Press, 2000) and Consumerism in Twentieth-Century Britain: The Search for a Historical Movement (Cambridge University Press, 2003). He is currently working on a project on the consumer in a global perspective.

Iselin Theien is a postdoctoral fellow in contemporary history at the University of Oslo, working on consumerism under social democracy. She is also affiliated to the Institute for Social Research, Oslo, where she has been researching the history of the Norwegian consumer co-operative movement in the period from 1920-55. She has a D.Phil in Modern History, with a thesis on Norwegian Fascism, from the University of Oxford.

Gunnar Trumbull is an assistant professor at Harvard Business School, where he teaches political economy. He earned his Ph.D. in political science from MIT, and his BA from Harvard College. He has worked as a researcher at the European University Institute and The Brookings Institution. His research focuses on European regulatory policy, including consumer protection and technology policy.

Jon Vatnaland took his cand. polit. degree in Sociology at the University of Oslo in 2002. He is currently a Ph.D student at the Centre for technology, innovation and culture at the University of Oslo and in 2004-2005 attend as Visiting Scholar at the Department of Sociology, University of California, Berkeley. Vatnaland has mainly been working with the development of retail chains and economic sociology. His most recent publication is the book *Næringslivet mellom marked og politikk*, which he co-authored with Espen Ekberg Fredrik Engelstad and Trygve Gulbrandsen (Engelstad et al. 2003).